THE EXPERTS RESPOND

"FINALLY a book that provides a first-hand lo[ok]
lege and the unfamiliar journey of the college e[...]
spective of private and public, small and large c[...]
the issues, reactions, and how they adjusted to [...]
students — insightful and eye opening! It's a r[...]
college (and parents, too) who wants to get t[...]
Read...learn...and survive the college shock!"

RENEE BARNETT TERRY, Ph[...]
Dean of Student Affairs
University of California – San D[...]

"Parents may not even think of these topics a[...]
lege. Leaving high school, however, and going [...]
transitions. College Shock is a useful guide t[...]
logue on many points.

I like this book. I am going to use it in my pra[...]

ELEANORE U. MEYER, M.D.
Adolescent Medicine
Santa Monica, CA

"We decided that College Shock would be the [...]
ter understand just what their residents are g[...]
the very helpful Study Strategies, Points to P[...]
in College Shock to help their freshman resid[...]
are excited about the intense and in-depth dis[...]
about what their resident students are going th[...]
with in College Shock. College Shock gives [...]
that our R.A.s might not have been able to hea[...]
to address. College Shock will help our upper[...]
help them to better serve our resident student [...]
they are going through from the first moment they [...]

JENNIFER ROY
Coordinator of Programming and [...]
California State University, Chico[...]

College Shock

How to Survive the First Year of College

Sally Landau and Val Holwerda
with contributing students

Bristol Press Inc.
Los Angeles

● ●

DEDICATION

To all the new college students out there.
Good Luck! And enjoy it while you can!

● ●

Finale from INTO THE WOODS
Music and Lyrics by Stephen Sondheim
Copyright© 1987, 1988, 1989 by Rilting Music Inc.
All Rights Administered by WB Music Corp.
All Rights Reserved Used by Permission

Publisher's Cataloging-in-Publication
(Provided by Quality Books, Inc.)

Landau, Sally.
    College shock : how to survive the first year of
college / Sally Landau and Val Holwerda with
contributing students. — 1st ed.
    p. cm.
    ISBN: 0-9629458-5-4

    1. Women—Education (Higher)—United States—
Handbooks, manuals, etc. 2. College student orientation
—United States—Handbooks, manuals, etc. 3. Women
college students—United States—Life skills guides.
I. Holwerda, Val. II. Title.

LC1757.L36 2001   378.1'9822
                           QBI01-201046

Design Assistance: Barbara Gottlieb, Brian White
Editing: Sara Fisher

Published by Bristol Press Inc., Post Office Box 49958, Los Angeles, CA 90049
www.promaris.com • **e-mail: collegeshock@promaris.com**
310.719.4053 • fax: 310.454.6474

Contents

● ●

INTRODUCTION

"Don't expect things to remain the same. I had never lived anywhere but [my home-town] until I moved to [college]. Settling in wasn't a problem, but I'm still in the process of adjusting. I don't know that anyone could have prepared me for how much I would have to grow up this past year. I never realized how much I had taken for granted, from things as minor as food quality — it's not fun eating canned preprocessed food <u>every</u> day — to significant eye openers like sometimes frightening insights into human nature. No one can stress enough how important it is to know who you are and to be open to change."

ARIELLE, during her sophomore year

The freshman experience has been so romanticized – by Hollywood and nostalgic parents alike – that the rose-colored glasses can sometimes get downright myopic. How can this grand event *not* get romanticized? It's a young person's first taste of unfettered freedom, frat parties and (possibly) beer. It's academics without a safety net, and the uniquely odd practice of being forced to share an insanely small room with at least one other total stranger. Soul mates are discovered, and those pesky "character-building lessons" that we wish we could skip are endured.

Freshman year is a carnival ride, two parts exhilaration and one part terror. **Every young woman interviewed for this book successfully survived her freshman year, but everyone also discovered that the way was filled with more than a few potholes and pitfalls.** It's one heck of a unique experience. Hold on and have a blast.

This book is the story of young women's transitions to college; the lowdown on what freshman year is really about. It attempts to unravel the key issues involved in entering and navigating that first year of college life, looking far beyond the classroom. This book is for the college-bound student and for the parent coping on the other end of the phone line and the checkbook.

The stories related herein are real, as are the young women who were interviewed. As students they are linked by the shared thread of having done very well in high school and matriculating to top American colleges and universities. The schools they selected, public and private, had especially outstanding reputations for retaining their freshman class and having the class graduate in four or so years.

The interviews were confidential, with the women choosing aliases for the book in return for speaking with absolute candor. Wow, did the stories pour forth. Even more incredible was the fact that these very different young women, camped out at very different colleges, shared many of the same frustrations and experiences. They even shared much of the same 20/20 hindsight-inspired advice. **The book is organized around the topics most frequently discussed by and solutions recommended by the young women themselves.** Yes, there is a bit of editorializing and some words of wisdom from a few generous experts. **But, by and large, this book comes straight from the interviewees.** Think of it as a kindred spirit to the Gettysburg Address – of, by and for college freshmen.

Some of the young women interviewed fastened their seatbelts and plunged ahead. Others made huge sacrifices, and others felt as if they were swimming upstream. **Most felt they emerged stronger for the experience.**

No matter how well prepared a high school student, no matter how extensive of an extracurricular life, no matter how many summers away from home at sleep-away camp, freshman years rarely play out as expected. The amazing, memories-of-a-lifetime experiences are there, and so are the events that can throw a young woman off her stride, perhaps to a minor degree, perhaps massively.

That's where this book comes in..

<u>College Shock</u> is a book to help you, students and parents alike, navigate through the newness and unfamiliarity that comes with this particular stretch of life's journey. We hope it helps. We think it will. We certainly wish we'd had it for the first college go-rounds in our families.

● ●

UP FRONT AND PERSONAL: *Yes, the Young Women are Real*

Yes, the young women quoted in this book are real college students scattered across the U.S.A. And yes, their names have been changed as well as the names of roommates and friends, hometowns, college majors, and class selections. Their freedom to speak openly without any hesitation was paramount. Each young woman selected her own alias, drawing inspiration from literary heroines and neighbors' dogs alike.

For more information on whose insights you're reading, check out Appendix A to get the run-down on the young women's scholastic backgrounds; authentic, and unchanged, but still anonymous.

And yes, the colleges are real as well. We promised not to pair the women with the colleges or universities they actually attended. Frequently and somewhat surprisingly, one student would extol the very aspect of a school (the core curriculum or vegetarian dining options, for example) that were the source of complaints for another young woman at the *very same* institution. It is all in the beholder's view. Overwhelmingly, the experiences of the young women are far more significant than the exact identity of the school. You will find (also in Appendix A) information about the size and setting of the schools being discussed so readers can better fit the women's comments into context.

Bottom line: This book tackles the *transitions* young women make during their first year in college. The key issue is not what school they attended, but how they reacted to and handled the big plunge into the collegiate world. Don't worry, nothing important was lost by fudging either the participants' or colleges' actual identities.

••••••••••••••••••••••••••••••••••••

Through
the
Looking Glass

Home is home – after all there's no place like it. It's familiar. It's predictable, be it your favorite Sunday breakfasts or the weekly sibling fights over hogging the bathroom. You have your recognized role there, with unquestioned talents and personality quirks. The security can be comforting or cloying, or most likely both.

Now it's off to college. Regardless of whether you were dying to leave home at age 15 or find yourself misty eyed as the summer before college races by, your entire world is going to be rocked. While every person's experience transitioning from home life to college life is unique, here is one guarantee – it's never exactly what you thought it would be. No matter how many advice books you poured over or alumnae you grilled, no matter how prepared you feel yourself to be, this is going to be an astounding, different experience than what you expected.

Fortunately, entering college is one life-event most universities recognize as requiring attention, nurturing and care. Freshmen are inundated with orientation gatherings, informational sessions and support structures. Use them. At the very least investigate everything offered. These early college experiences can be a total blast. If nothing else, they will ease the transition, guaranteed.

Regardless, this transition time will be filled with befuddling Cheshire Cats, seemingly hostile Queens, and incomprehensible tea parties. Expectations versus reality will duel, all the while you try to forge a new identity for yourself. So hold on to your hats, it's going to be one heck of a bumpy – but fascinating – ride.

ORIENTEERING

Every college in this nation offers freshman orientations, but that's about where the similarities end. Some have camping or rafting trips held during the summer to give a first glimpse of your new classmates, as well as to build trust and friendships. Others offer more bare-bones affairs that let Resident Advisors (R.A.s) chat with residents-to-be. Some events occur in the middle of the summer; most are held during the time-honored Freshman Orientation Week right before classes start. (Enjoy the campus during these days, since it's the only time freshmen rule the roost.) During those days, most colleges will offer a schedule crammed with ice cream socials, academic counseling, outings to the local college town or nearest city, dorm pajama parties, and a chance to meet representatives from campus organizations.

Sound exhausting? It is. But it also provides a group of unique activities that while not required, should be experienced if at all humanly possible. The young women interviewed who took advantage of these early events largely reported much easier transitions. They also reported that what they got out of the experience was directly correlated to what they put into it.

There is one overriding suggestion here. Do everything – the good, the bad, the seemingly boring. You will probably hit some dud events, although even those young women who attended unsuccessful events met some people, which took the edge off the alien feeling of the initial college experience. You may just as likely stumble upon the kind of event that legendary freshmen memories are made of. So take your chances and go!

Here are the tales of young women and how they fared. Think through your actions and reactions, and how you would/could/did respond.

Fortunately for **Lola,** who did not know a soul and had never seen her 3,000-mile-away-from-home campus, her university sponsored a week-long, mandatory orientation period immediately prior to the fall semester. There were lots of activities, including school wide events and dorm-only outings. She had a chance to get to know her roommate before the stress of school kicked in. The orientation even scheduled time for taking care of mundane details – like starting her e-mail account and registering for a residence hall mailbox –

which surprisingly was fun since Lola was surrounded by her new peers. For Lola, the orientation week was an absolute lifeline.

Kate also had a good orientation experience. She chose to go on a wilderness retreat, which turned out to be a blast. Although she was attending an ultra-large, somewhat impersonal university, the school made a real effort to help freshmen connect. And connect Kate did – by making friends and even meeting Matthew, who became That Special Someone. By the time school started, Kate was already surrounded by friends and had built good memories plus a boyfriend to boot.

Then there was **Ayla**, who attended the same school as Kate. She opted not to go on any of the offered wilderness trips and community service outings, choosing instead to attend an academic orientation at the end of the summer. The tedious two-day event was valuable when it came to pragmatic matters like financial aid and class selection, but it did little to bring the new students together in a social setting. Only 10 people showed up to a barbecue, and the final nail in the coffin of this unsuccessful event was a mandatory 9:00 p.m. curfew.

Ayla tried again during the freshman welcome week, when some social events were offered. None was too successful, however. One afternoon she went to play pool at a well-publicized event. She found only tables – no balls, no cue sticks, and no people! *"At first I thought I was just nervous, like everyone else."* Ayla ultimately left this powerhouse public university and is happy in her new, more intimate school setting. Looking back, Ayla felt that although her decision to leave the larger school was inevitable, she should have gone to all the orientations, and would have done things differently if she could do it over again.

Karen's experience lies somewhere in the middle of the spectrum. She signed up for a three-day wilderness trip, for which she had very high expectations about meeting lifelong friends from the get-go. The expedition was fine. She had a nice time, and became friendly with the students she met – but her expectations, logical or not, were not met. Karen took a deep breath and got over the disappointment. She says she was still glad she went, since there were at least some friendly faces on the first days of school.

> **"**
> **At first
> I thought
> I was
> just nervous,
> like
> everyone else.
> "**
>
> AYLA

Points to Ponder

1. Sign up! Participate! Explore!
2. Be open-minded (Sound familiar?)
3. Consider the glass half full. Try not to burden yourself with high expectations.
4. Regardless of what happens, mentally move on.

MOVE-IN DAY

This is the college cliché Hollywood loves most when it comes to the movies. Exterior setting: a weathered college dorm, with SUVs stuffed to the gills being unloaded by eager kids and red-eyed parents. Interior setting: A total zoo. Smiling and eager students rush around with armloads of possessions jostling in the elevator, and both empty and full boxes spill down the hall. Finale: Parents give one last look around the tiny room that is to be their baby's new home, nearly smother their child with hugs and kisses before tear-fully pulling away, and give last-minute dorky advice until the new freshman pushes them out the door.

Then there is reality. Not surprisingly, Hollywood is often way off the mark.

Arielle thought her parents would make a fuss before departing. ***"I thought they would make a big deal about saying good-bye."*** Surprise. On the way to a barbecue, they simply turned and said they would be leaving. And they *did!* It took Arielle's breath away. She felt let down, and somewhat abandoned in a throw-your-baby-in-the-pool school of swimming way.

Allison's parents flew 3,000 miles with her to help her get settled into her new campus home. There was an enormous flurry of activity. Then, once her computer was set up, boxes tucked under her bed, and closet meticulously arranged, her parents left and it was very, very quiet. ***"Well, OK. The most difficult part was when my parents left. Pretty grim."***

Of course, Arielle and Allison survived. No matter what their particular methods, your parents are going to evaporate at some point. Then what? It is one thing to be packed and unpacked with the help of your parents or other loved ones, and quite another to finally face your new campus home all alone. That moment always comes, too.

Points to Ponder

Be prepared. This is generally one of life's gut-wrenching moments. Bring Kleenex.

What else will help? How about Ben and Jerry's? Better yet, get involved with what is offered. The colleges know this is a tough time and will have organized events to help out. Or, simply walk around your dorm until you find someone with their door open and no parents in sight. Go in and introduce yourself.

EARLY TRAUMAS AND OTHER SURPRISES

No matter how much pre-planning and guidance counselor hand-holding, as the school year cranks up to full steam, it's very likely that you'll get caught in some sort of maelstrom. It can easily grow wildly out of control if you let it. Moreover, you may create your own trauma (or drama) in the countless expectations you either knowingly or unknowingly brought with you to college. Reality simply isn't going to live up.

So, what do you do? Here's just a suggestion: First, breathe deeply, cry if you have to, and hunt down chocolate in needed quantities. Then attend to your business. Unlike high school, you're on your own to sort out problems. Resist the urge to call Mom right away. Make a list of what has to be done, prioritize and figure out plans of attack. You'll be fine, promise.

Sift through these early experiences that some women encountered, and see how you would have handled the factors involved. Would you have been flexible enough to handle the issues and the consequences? Would you have tackled the issue another way?

Lauren had a truly first horrendous week. Her requested class schedule was not granted, with school administrators saying her enrollment papers never arrived. She was assigned to a graduate-student residence hall and all the wrong classes. Her desired classes were full.

> Like most of the interviewees, Lauren was bright, well-prepared, and eager to conquer her new life. She just wasn't quite ready for the welcome from hell. Persistent to the end, however, Lauren first marched over to the housing guru. Unfortunately, he was only a sophomore – well-intentioned and *"cute,"* but unable to help. She put dorm life on hold for the time being and made a priority of getting aca-

"
The most difficult part was when my parents left. Pretty grim.
"
ALLISON

demics under control. She marched off to registration central, where bureaucratic lines twisted up stairwells and down hallways. Then she headed off to petition individual teachers. She met with her advisor and lugged her portfolio to show to her desired art professor. This process lasted during the entire orientation and first week of classes. But after all this work, *voilà*, Lauren emerged with a schedule to her satisfaction. Ever the optimist, she even observed that thanks to this nightmare, she got a leg up in getting to know her professors. Somewhere along the way, even the housing problem was solved. She switched to a cheery freshman residence hall filled with more kindred souls.

P.S.: Think this happened at a large public university, where you are just a number? Well, Lauren had just matriculated to one of the best private schools in the country with a reputation for a low student-faculty ratio and a sterling national reputation.

Sydney summed it all up when she observed that in college *"you can't get all your information from one person. Instead you have to seek out the help of perhaps twelve."*

Unfortunately, **Alexandra's** hard times were mostly of her own creation. She had incredibly high hopes for her small college, most of which were not met. She was disappointed with a class she had chosen solely by its title in the catalogue, "Math as it Relates to Art," thinking it to would relate to virtual art on the computer. It wasn't, and she hated it. Then she fought with her only friend at school, and they stopped speaking. A depression of sorts set in, and she went on Prozac – albeit for only two days.

Alexandra spoke to her parents, who were supportive overall. Her mom counseled against taking anti-depressants, and both parents encouraged her to come home if she was that unhappy. Alexandra seriously considered transferring to a local university, or even her mom's alma mater. *"I wasn't up for the process of applying,"* she finally decided, and claimed a general loyalty and an interest in wanting *"to give it a try."* So she stuck it out, although she moaned when looking back over her disconcerting first semester. *"I felt like I was on that boat ride in* **Willy Wonka and The Chocolate Factory."** How would you have handled Alexandra's crisis?

Points to Ponder

Expect turmoil. The university begins anew each year, and to some extent each semester or quarter. The transitions won't necessarily be smooth, no matter how well intentioned or bright the powers-that-be.

Some of your expectations probably won't be realized. You came to learn, right? How's this for a learning experience – some of what you are expecting may not materialize. Time to accept and deal with it. This is part of your new life.

You'll be changing too. Be prepared for this as well. It's part of the dynamic and the excitement of college.

DOWN THE RABBIT HOLE

You've got the dorm situation under control, you're content with your class schedule, and your social life is starting to take off. Shouldn't college be smooth sailing from here? Don't bet on it. Unfortunately, freshmen seem to almost universally experience the emotional equivalent of tumbling down the rabbit hole. For want of a better word, let's call it rootlessness. It's a pesky little inner-voice that peevishly suggests you're a tad out of place, that you're just not quite your same old self here, or that no one knows the real you. Even worse, what *is* the real you?

Face it, high school glory days are over. In high school, everyone crafts an identity for themselves, where they have their activities and are known as stars in certain areas. Then you get to college, and no one knows your perfect debating record or your state-final wins for track. No one may care, and even harder to accept, they may have the same or *better* achievements.

The flip side of this phenomenon is the liberating, if somewhat destabilizing, realization that you can leave old activities behind and pursue entirely new ones. The opportunity to forge a successful track record in entirely new and surprising directions is wonderful, but some women interviewed can't quite shake the feeling that they aren't being entirely true to themselves.

While every student had different experiences, most reported this sense of rootlessness – this 'who am I' crisis, if you will, or as our sociologist friends describe it, anomie. Read on and see how rootlessness manifested itself for these young women.

When **Simone** landed at college, she immediately started searching for girlfriends who would be just like her high school pals. It took her weeks to realize that exact cloning would be fruitless. More importantly, she stopped to think

> **"**
> *You can't get all your information from one person ...you have to seek out the help of perhaps twelve.*
> **"**
> SYDNEY

about why she was going about making friends this way. To her, at her great college with the prescription for success so obviously presented to her, Simone feared not fitting in. She felt so isolated and so friendless that she was looking to repeat the past.

"Being with all these people who are supposed to be like you - bright, ambitious, the future leaders of the world, as we are so graciously referred, and feeling so awkward. Not knowing how to make friends with these people when everyone tells you college is the time of your life," were some of Simone's overriding feelings. *"I certainly wasn't having the time of my life at the beginning."*

Simone described herself as *"having an identity crisis."* How people saw her was who she became in their eyes. She was used to the predictability of having had some of the same friends since kindergarten. This newness and feeling she had to prove herself over and over was foreign to her. And she didn't like it one bit.

.....Then the classes she took became defining characteristics in her identity. She became wrapped up in the ideas and mores presented in lectures, further losing the person she thought she was.

Next stop, some long-distance complaining. Her mom encouraged her to stick it out. In late October, Simone met two great friends, young women with passions similar to Simone's. Her new life began to take shape.

Lola dealt with a very specific and not-uncommon fear: that *"they made a mistake in the admissions department."* What in blazes was she doing at this school? Lola felt that other students appeared so much more stellar, more qualified than she. She was meeting fellow students who were published authors, holders of prestigious internships, multilingual wizards, inventors, and children and grandchildren of world leaders and royalty.

It took a while, but Lola no longer felt like a stowaway. The answer emerged in the classroom, where she found common ground. A highly motivated student, Lola found that most of her fellow freshmen were just as enthusiastic as she – and that they all had much more in common than she originally imagined. Lola has come to feel very much at home at her top-notch college.

For **Sara**, there was just one gut-wrenching conundrum: *"It is hard to admit that there are ups and downs. 'How are you doing' is a greeting to which the answer is an automatic 'great!' So it seems like everyone is having a great time except you. Over Christmas that first year, I met people who said to me 'these are the best years of your life.' Well isn't that depressing. You feel like a loser when you feel the downs that in fact everybody feels. You ask yourself, 'what am I doing wrong?'"*

This is where people's façades can become shaky. Taking a step back from the situation, it's easy to realize that of course a lot of students will put a positive spin on things. (How many casual acquaintances would ever truthfully answer, "I'm a total mess and miss my dog?")

It's also easy to realize that some adults will put a rosy spin on certain freshman memories. Ultimately, Sara got past appearances and realized that her fellow students felt the same way she did. She became calmer. She connected with new friends. Time passed, and college became home.

Harriet had the most succinct turn of phrase. ***"In college, the shell cracks and the egg decides what it will become."***

Scarlett's personal rabbit hole turned out to be a complete change in extracurricular activities. Like many – if not most – freshmen, her interests shifted. As a gymnast in high school, she practiced 20 hours each week and attended meets on the weekends. Yet she simply slipped away from the sport when she arrived at college. To her surprise, the college newspaper captured her attention. Scarlett had spent a lot of time reading college papers when investigating college choices, since they revealed unparalleled insights into campus life, but she had no intention of pursuing journalism. Much to her own surprise, however, she quickly fell into writing for her campus paper, and is now a featured op-ed writer. Perhaps her college selection had more to do with the campus newspaper than she ever imagined.

Points to Ponder

Feelings of rootlessness generally emerge. Try not to let these strong emotions turn you inside out. This is an acclimation process that will take time. You will manage it beautifully, and emerge with a better idea of who you really are. Which leads to …

Be ready to discover your new self. It will be right there waiting inside the old you. Prediction: these two selves are going to be good friends.

THE UGLY TRUTH ABOUT FREEDOM

Most teens spend their adolescence nudging, begging and perhaps even whining for more independence. It's natural. After all, they consider themselves to be adults. And if most

"
*I felt
like I was
on that
boat ride
in*
**Willy Wonka
and
The Chocolate
Factory.**
"
ALEXANDRA

college-bound women had to sum up college with one word, it very well may be 'freedom.' Freedom to lead lives the way they want; the freedom to make their own decisions, large and small. Then they get to college, taste the freedom … and freak? Who ever knew that there would be a downside to independence?

Simone related her personal paradox: *"…emotionally it was bizarre. The first time you realize you're alone, it's exciting, spiritually freeing, like 'no one cares what I do.' Then you realize with an awkward sadness, 'no one cares what I do.'"*

A conversation with Sam

Q. So, Sam, what made you feel good?

A. *"Realizing I was happier at college."*

Q. And, what made you feel bad?

A. *"Realizing I was happier at college."*

Q. Anything else?

A. *"I have no idea where I'm going, and I used to know."*

Sam described awakening to the reality of *"no security blanket."* There was no one there to pick up lunch if the refrigerator was empty and the dining hall was closed. No one would drop off the paper she forgot to tuck in her backpack. She had only herself to blame for going hungry, and only she could trudge for almost an hour back and forth across a windswept campus. Also, there was no one to nurse her through a case of flu. It gave a whole new meaning to being on your own.

Looking back, Sam realized that loneliness crept in *"when I felt I wasn't taking advantage of the college experience. The realization of happiness became obvious when I caught myself and realized that I loved school."*

Of course, while there are downsides, the sheer joy of freedom seemed to ultimately prevail. **Alexandra** was the most direct. *"I was born to be free!"* **Scarlett,** too, loves the *"freedom to do whatever, whenever."*

Points to Ponder

The Yin and Yang of Freedom. It has two sides: sweet and sour, delicious and scary. You're gonna love the fun side, but discover that the other side can be frightening. (The ever-dramatic Janis Joplin *did* say something about freedom being just another word for nothing left to lose.) Loneliness will intrude, and perhaps a feeling of spinning a bit out of control. But remember, you're still loved by those who loved you before. Don't be afraid to let them know that you still need them. Also, previous thoughts hold true: Be prepared to discover your new self-struggling to emerge.

In the end, it worked! All the young women interviewed clicked their heels in glee at the independence college life brought. It just took time to adjust, but they all lived happily ever after. Odds are, you will too.

THERE'S NO INNOCULATION FOR HOMESICKNESS

The good news is that tales of homesickness were few and far between. The downside, however, is that when homesickness hits, it can be ugly. For the reported cases, most homesickness was characterized as temporary. Bouts largely occurred during the early fall, and lasted for just a month or two. Believe it or not, some young women even described homesickness as constructive. It helped them better understand themselves, and prompted them to forge good friendships with new people. Some even appreciated their homes and families better as their parents cheer leaded them through the rough times.

Missing her home terribly, **Jane** called her parents daily. *"I was really, really homesick, and that was a huge shock to me. I'd never been [homesick] before."* Looking for help at school discouraged her. She felt that *"kids in college can't be supportive; they're all in the same place."*

Insomnia struck. The days became increasingly difficult, and her concentration level declined. Jane tried to catch up on sleep during the days, which only kept her up later at night. Fortunately she had great support from her family, and could call them any time day or night. And did!

Encouraged both at home and at her prep school to be independent and self-sufficient, Jane finally realized that it would have to be she who took charge of her life. *"I'm going to pull myself out of this. I gave myself a kick in the butt."* She began taking walks for exercise, forced herself to get up early (and attend every class), and she started seeing her soon-to-be boyfriend, Peter. While other issues arose before she reached college nirvana, Jane did take the first steps towards overcoming her homesickness and started on a better path.

For **Simone,** homesickness descended during the first week. Quite irrationally, she just wanted to return to high school. She missed everyone and everything. She called home in tears. What she really missed was a familiar atmosphere where she could be her old self, protected from others' judgments and the new challenges hurdling her way.

College wasn't the first time Simone was away from home; she had attended sleep-away camp for three summers. But this was different. Going away to college was being grown up. *"The first two months were a series of lonely evenings; Sunday afternoons and meals surrounded by people you pretended to know."*

Then, with the support of her family and her new friends, the homesickness part of her adjustment evaporated. It took a few months, and not all the problems went away, but life grew to be much better.

Sara's homesickness came simply from missing her family. It was hard for her to have relationships by phone, and to be a big sister to a little brother in such an abstract way. Celebrating her birthday 3,000 miles from home was poignant, but new friends made it bearable and ultimately fun.

Sometimes it's the little things that get you down. **Lindsay** acknowledged *"I felt homesick… when I was sick."*

Ann reported *"Sometimes I get a little homesick around the breaks when most people are away and I stay on campus."*

Points to Ponder

Take it as it comes. Homesickness does pass. Follow up with these points to move the feelings of homesickness off your emotional scorecard.

Expect homesickness. Then it won't be a shock if it raises its ugly head. Realize homesickness is a natural part of your transition to college. Remember that it usually is temporary.

Expect this homesickness to be different than going away to summer camp. It feels more permanent because it *is* more permanent. You're growing up. It could also affirm your great, happy childhood and this new awareness that you have moved on to the next stage of life. And if homesickness never appears, think how well-prepared you were to leave home and experience this new life.

Keep looking for friends. They're out there. Consider all your options (clubs, residence hall affiliations, intramural sports, the laundry room and on and on) and go for it.

Create a comfort zone. Once the glamour of sudden freedom wears off, some of the most successful transitions were a result of creating a routine out of chaos, then pretty much sticking to it. Of course the serendipity of what is offered is what makes college special. It's a tricky balance, but one you'll learn to manage.

Should the feelings overwhelm you, seek help. R.A.s, professors, counselors, clergy, parents, classmates and more are all in your life to support you. Really. Ask for help.

SMORGASBORD

The following is a collection of smaller and more individualized – but no less real – problems that the young women faced in their new college life.

A small-town college town. Meredith's biggest problem was that her college town was *too* small-town. Coming from a big city, Meredith never gave a thought to just how small a small town could be until she landed in one. She still shakes her head as she recounts a shopping trip to a local discount store. After purchasing her needed basics, the clerk asked if she needed help out to her car. As they walked out, the clerk inquired which of the two nearby colleges she attended. At her answer, the clerk dropped her purchases at the curb and spun away on his heel. Meredith was left standing, astonished. Why exactly? Meredith never figured it out. For some long forgotten reason the school she attends was stigmatized; the store clerk echoed the sentiments of many in the town.

So while college life was fabulous, Meredith found the town oppressive in its negativity and intolerance. While it wasn't a reason to transfer, she was still caught by surprise by this unpleasantness. Meredith chose from here on out to avoid the town, which makes her school feel a bit more claustrophobic, but for her this was the best strategy.

> **"**
> *I certainly wasn't having the time of my life at the beginning.*
> **"**
> SIMONE

Worry, worry, worry. Anne B.'s mode of operation was constant worry when she first arrived at college. *"How my parents would survive, friends, roommates, you name it, I worried about it."* This can be an understandable but exhausting way to live. As Anne acclimated, her obsessive worrying died down to a more manageable level. She still talks to her mom nightly, but feels that by now she (and her mom) has made the transition completely. The road to comfort seems to have taken about a month, which is a timeframe commonly reported by many students.

Divorce *now*? Charlotte faced a major turning point her freshman year, which other young women mentioned as well. Just upon leaving for college, Charlotte's parents' marriage dissolved. While divorce has become commonplace in many lives, it is none the less devastating – whether it happens when the children are two or 20. Moreover, Charlotte's parents decided to sell their house, meaning that come vacation time, she had no home to which to return.

Charlotte's parents' divorce forced her to find refuge in school. New friends at college offered great support as she realized that her family, the linchpin of her life, had crumbled. Somewhat ironically, by comparison, her transition to college seemed smooth. Out of necessity, her school became her home. A negative became a positive.

The Nitty-gritties. Sara's significant problem turned out to be the mundane minutiae of everyday life. Running out of toothpaste. Nothing to eat. Being sick and alone. Dealing with the bank. Paying her own phone bills. It took time, but she finally sorted out this necessary stuff.

Sort-of sexism. Sam's major transitional issue was an unexpected gender issue. Having graduated from a top-notch girls' school that empowered her academically and psychologically, Sam found herself surprisingly ill-prepared for coed life. Wherever she looked, she felt different and alone. *"It was difficult to be with girls who didn't go to an all girls' school."* Sam checked out the sorority system, then rushed and pledged. Then she thought about it some more and de-pledged. Moving away from yet another all girls' environment was part of her growth. It took time, but today she feels strong and comfortable in the co-ed scenario called life.

> **" [I was afraid] they made a mistake in the admissions department. "**
>
> LOLA

Unholy weather. For Lola, weather proved an unforeseen hitch. Coming from a warm climate at home, the severe change in her college town was quite a shock at first. *"Scheduling an 8:00 a.m. Spanish class was a big mistake."* Lola learned that the walk across campus at that hour was unearthly cold.

Leila found the weather to be a more serious problem. California born and bred, Leila already felt different from many of her classmates in dress, attitude, and philosophies.

However, initial transition to school was easy. What proved to be a major stumbling block, however, was the weather. Serious winter chills took hold all too soon, and with it the new experience of stuffing herself into countless layers of clothes, then sweltering in tank-tops in over-heated classrooms, only to repeat the clothing process before running to her next class. Partying, studying, eating and socializing all, out of necessity, suddenly were indoor activities. Leila felt out of place. She hated everything about an East Coast winter, and realized for the first time just how much she needed the great outdoors. Her East Coast university was suffocating her. Ultimately, Leila left for warmer climates.

Sara's reaction to the weather had a name: Seasonal Affective Disorder (S.A.D.). The health service staff knew all about it and they were helpful. The primary symptom was depression. It seemed to affect most students plucked from sunny climates, especially that first semester. Sara survived, of course, but it wasn't the easiest experience to get through.

Loneliness. Having been through many changes and evolutions since college began, **Ayla** experienced what she called loneliness. Emphasizing the silver lining, Ayla had an upbeat spin on loneliness. *"Feeling lonely has been a positive experience. You can be surrounded by people and still feel lonely, but it shapes you if you embrace it. You can become your own person."*

Clinical Depression. For **Harriet**, something felt quite wrong her second semester of college. After sailing through the first semester on a high like summer camp, an old feeling revisited Harriet after winter break. She realized for the first time, compared to the joy of the last semester, just how unhappy she was, and how unhappy she had been. She had first felt that there may be a problem back in high school, but she was not officially diagnosed with depression until her freshman year. She went to the school health services, who referred her to a private doctor. He gave her the frightening diagnosis of severe depression, which made her even more depressed. But Harriet went on medication, which helped immensely, as did the support from her family. Harriet reportedly believes heredity has at least played a part in her illness, and hoped that she could go off the medication within two years or so.

And now I'm moving out of the dorm. Flush with freedom, 3,000 miles apart, **Ayla** and **Holden** didn't even know each other, made the same decision, and the same mistake. As their respective freshman years edged to a close, both decided to move off campus and each selected new homes that

> **"**
> *Scheduling*
> *an*
> *8:00 a.m.*
> *Spanish class*
> *was a*
> *big mistake.*
> **"**
>
> LOLA

were way out of the mainstream. For Ayla this meant buying a car to get to class and being isolated from ready access to friends. For Holden it meant long walks at night to get home, finding escorts, or just leaving the library, the party or whatever, early. Either way it was a hassle to say nothing of losing their top-notch computer hookups. But each girl swore by off-campus housing. Each subsequently moved to a newer off-campus home that is closer to the action. Might want to think of these stories when you get the gotta-get-off-campus itch.

SOMETIMES IT'S EASY

After this laundry list of potential pitfalls, remember that sometimes the transition to university life is just plain easy. That was the case for **Amber**. Having had several summer camp experiences and a jammed schedule of after-school activities, Amber was quite independent. She found acclimating to college life a natural process. *"I felt ready to leave home."* She also found that establishing a routine gave her a sense of belonging and serenity. There was a whirlwind beginning. Then Amber settled into regular sleep patterns, regular mealtimes, established study times, and relentless attendance in class.

Kate, too, found the transition effortless. Kate was gentle with herself and comfortable inside herself. She was pleasantly surprised to find a decreased workload from her pedal-to-the-metal prep school. And even though she is incredibly close to her mother, and even chose a school because of its proximity to her home, she did not find it difficult to leave the nest. *"I was so ready for college."*

These women were lucky, and it can just as likely be you.

"
In college, the shell cracks and the egg decides what it will become.
"
HARRIET

MOST REPEATED ADVICE AWARD

"Getting involved in school and campus activities is so important. Get to know people and be active. Any way you can use your time constructively and have fun and meet people helps a lot."
— **Karen,** and paraphrased by many others.

● ●

EASING THE TRANSITION

Here you go, the insta-version of this chapter.

Go to every possible orientation. Or at least, as many as possible. Especially make time for the fun ones. Mingle. Explore. Have fun. If you hit a dud, move on.

Be prepared for early mix-ups. Go into battle with your entire arsenal prepped: analysis, persuasion, information, tears, bravado, manipulation, and downright bullying. Maybe flirting. There's a lot you can do. So get on with it. Don't let 'em get you down, and don't let yourself feel helpless.

Expect that out-of-place feeling. Rootlessness can be depressing, but know that in all likelihood many of your new friends and neighbors are experiencing the exact same feelings. Be prepared to recognize this slippery emotion. You'll be absolutely fine in the long run.

Expect a bit of terror with all this new freedom and independence. It can be scary, but it can be the start of something marvelous. You'll have lots more free time in college. No more back-to-back classes and a six-deep course load. Be purposeful and creative, the traits that earned you your college berth. Take a deep breath. Explore. Freedom and independence will soon be a comfortable part of your new life.

Be prepared for the possibility of temporary friendlessness. Expect a merry-go-round of friends in the whirlwind beginning. High school friends are scattered, and miss you as much as you do them. You'll make and drift apart from new found friends. Some will stay; some will go. True friends will emerge in time.

Conquer the details. Make a list of chores, set aside time, and go to it! Buy toothpaste, get checks cashed (open a checking account), make deposits, buy healthy snacks. These issues aren't going to go away, and no one else will take care of you, so don't try to pull an ostrich act.

Figure out a routine. An orderly way of living will bring a measure of tranquility and a reassuring pace to your new life.

Figure out your roommate issues. Make a happy, or at least peaceful home. Take a minute and read the roommate chapter.

If you get sick, you're going to get feel lonely, deserted, sad, or angry. Or maybe all of them. Anticipate it, let yourself briefly wallow in it and pamper yourself. Call Mom. Order chicken soup from a local takeout restaurant. Let friends help you. Let acquaintances help you – maybe they'll become friends. And don't forget the Golden Rule: Be ready to help others when needed.

The weather. Be prepared. The changes in the weather might affect you more that you expected.

Re-entry woes. Sorry to say, it's going to be tough returning home at Thanksgiving. If you think going away to school is difficult, wait for the re-entry. Be sure to think about this as you take off for Turkey Day. In fact, there is a whole chapter on just what others found. Put a note in your daybook or organizer to check it out come mid-November.

Read the following sub chapter with Stephanie's story. It is a good overview. Think how you will handle all these issues. All at once.

• •

STEPHANIE'S STORY: A BUMPY TRANSITION

Stephanie's high school experience verged on the charmed. She did it all, and did it all well. Violinist. Pianist. Sprinter. Cheerleader. Starting center on her Varsity Basketball team. Social life. Academics. Life was good.

Then came college, and the transition proved to be the emotional equivalent of running full-force into a brick wall. For a myriad of reasons, many her fault and many not, her chosen university did not live up to expectations. Yes, Stephanie kept plowing ahead and ultimately made her peace with the college, but emerged with some strong opinions on how her transition could have been easier, better, faster, smarter. See what she had to say. How would you have handled these issues?

The problems started in the selection process. Stephanie 'fesses up: At least some of her problems were the fall-out from less than methodical methods in selecting a school. She wished that she had made a detailed pros and cons list for each college, delving more closely into what schools offered and what she could offer in return to each school.

The view book. During the selection process, Stephanie looked at the view book and liked what she saw. But once a real live freshman, in the midst of it all, she looked back and realized the view book had some glaring flaws. Yes, it presented the positive images of the school and did so honestly. Yet, like all marketing material (which a view book is at its core), there were some convenient oversights. Recent campus developments that affected her directly had been ignored. The student union, a central meeting place that had been described in glowing terms, was actually in the middle of a renovation that would take at least another year. The residence halls, which were in serious need of renovation themselves, had unlucky overflow students living in the lounges. The school simply lacked places to hang out.

The core curriculum, which was heavily praised in the view book, fell short of its promise. In reality: *"...the choices [the selections] are lacking."* Even more frustrating was the fact that several core requirements were offered in the same time slot, forcing students to pick one and wait for the others to come round again. Stephanie believed that the school was in crisis, and *"it doesn't know what it wants to be."* Unfortunately, these insights would never be found in a view book.

The scheduling. Arriving on campus, Stephanie had a wicked surprise. She found that not only were freshman classes predetermined, they were back-to-back without a break.

Just like high school. This probably had been revealed beforehand, but Stephanie missed that memo. It was unwelcome news to her, and at this point Stephanie considered transferring.

Ultimately she decided to remain. Her intention was to double major in Sociology and Pre-Med. She knew that the specialized, upper-division classes would be more satisfying. She also weighed the fact that graduating from this highly regarded university would help boost her chances of getting into the medical school of her choice. But while she toiled through core requirements as a sophomore, those rewards seemed a long way off.

The attitude. The acclaimed professors were also a first-week disappointment. Quite shockingly, she found them to be sexist and uncaring, and Stephanie felt discriminated against by some. She noted with an undercurrent of anger that *"[this university] does not exist separate from the United States."* Discrimination is not acceptable in any form, anywhere. Stephanie's antidote was hard work and involvement in activities beyond academics. She sang with a gospel choir and tutored high school students. She had good friends, who supported her. Yet she was still disappointed with her experience.

The escape valve. With her disappointing introduction to higher academia, Stephanie felt that schoolwork was something to simply get out of the way. One incredibly easy way to accomplish this was to skip her classes and stay in her dorm room. Not surprisingly, her grades were sub-par her first semester freshman year. This prompted the sobering realization that she may not make it through school, her worst fear. Suddenly, skipping classes didn't seem as insignificant as it had at first. *"You realize it later, say, when grades drop."* Stephanie then attended classes diligently, and saw her grades rebound up accordingly.

The roommate. When it came to her roommate, it at first looked like a good match-up. Stephanie felt she learned a lot from Nina, who came from a very different cultural background, and they were good friends. That was the first semester. Second semester, however, the two had a massive argument over an issue of great importance to both these (self-admitted) *"stubborn women."* They unhappily stuck out the remainder of the year together.

For her sophomore year, Stephanie was put on a housing list and assigned a new roommate. They got along, but an older-and-wiser Stephanie said, *"Let's see second semester."* She has also escaped from the meal plan, and bought and cooked her own food in her dorm kitchen. She planned to live in a dorm for four years; as a junior she would have priority, and hopefully land a single.

Moving on. Stephanie recognized that she was growing as a person. She continued to observe her world and take from it, perhaps reticently at times but with a growing sense of joy. She had an ongoing interest in political philosophy. She considered herself liberal, with a mounting interest in minority issues and the underprivileged. Overall, Stephanie evaluated her time at the university as worthwhile, but felt she should have looked deeper before she made her college choice.

•••••••••••••••••••••••••••••••••••••

"Is That My Sweater?" And Other Roommate Tales

Unseen university forces wave their magic wands, and – presto – a roommate duo (or trio) is born. Thrown together in good faith by their college, two women suddenly face each other from their respective sides of the room united by one burning question: Will this be the start of a beautiful friendship or the beginning of World War III?

Meeting your freshman roommate has to be one of the more anxiety-producing elements of the already staggering leap out of the home nest and into college life. You've filled out your college's roommate questionnaire - which can range from a half-page that focuses on the bare basics to a three-page manifesto that gets down to your favorite types of Friday night movies - but who knows what the reality will be? To make matters even more nerve wracking, most college-bound young women place enormous emphasis on their new roommate. **Holden,** who attends a top-tier private university, is far from alone when saying she was *"scared that bad housing would ruin my entire college experience."*

Well, good news and bad! Odds are your freshman roommate isn't going to be a joined-at-the-hip, pledged-godmother-to-your-unborn-child best friend. But the odds are just as strong that this young woman isn't going to be the total nightmare about whom urban legends and Hollywood movies are made. Most likely, your experience will be somewhere in the middle, with ups and downs **just like any relationship.** After all, your college has just taken two bright people, thrown them almost arbitrarily together in a very small room for nine months, and declared them well matched friends.

As **Jane** pointed out, *"I'm sorry to say that putting two strangers in a tiny space is just weird."*

No argument there. But weird can be fun; it can be enlightening; and it is guaranteed to be challenging. Even though most of the young women had previously lived away from home with relative strangers at summer camps, or shared a bathroom with a bratty brother, roommate dynamics are much different. For example, if there are problems, the battleground most typically forms in the second semester. The first semester is a honeymoon period, during which the new roommates don't say what is *really* on their minds.

This chapter on roommates is the book's longest by far. The women who were interviewed had more to say about roommates than anything else – including guys, sex or classes. Following are real-life scenarios which most roommates will face at some point. Keep in mind that these are real people with real flaws, which means you may disagree with or dislike some of their attitudes. However, the lessons remain the same. Read these stories and see how you would have handled these tricky situations.

THREE CAN BE A CROWD

Regardless of what college you attend, what roommate you get, and what your take is on relationships, it is guaranteed that at some point your room will not be big enough for you, your roommate, your roommate's significant other, or your significant other. Or all four of you. But while the specter of s-e-x can spark innumerable types of tension, the best solution is often the same. There are worthwhile thoughts shared here.

At first, **Ayla** was glad to be rooming with Nora, who shared her strong Christian upraising and ideals. But then they got to know each other. *"When I got there, I discovered Nora was a-n-a-l! One day I was working at the computer, and I leaned back and kissed my boyfriend. She ran for her Bible and read it for half an hour."* Even worse, most of Ayla's friends were guys, and Nora was unhappy whenever one of them came by to hang out. Ayla came to feel that she could never have friends over to her room to visit.

The roommates' discomfort mounted, but neither wanted to confront the issue – that is, until the end of the first quarter. The tension reached an unbearable level. The women finally talked openly about what was bugging them. From there, they figured out solutions they both could live with. Guidelines and rules about guests were set, and both agreed on some compromises. Ayla became more discrete. Nora loosened up. The two ultimately developed a respectful and long-lasting friendship, but it certainly was rough going in the beginning.

Then there is **Harriet,** and her roommate's boyfriend who wouldn't leave. Harriet and Jill got along remarkably well, but Jill's boyfriend of two years stayed the night as often as five nights a week. Jill and The Boyfriend completely ignored Harriet, acted as if she wasn't there, and pushed the levels of, ahem, discretion on their activities. Harriet ended up crashing in other dorm mates' rooms.

Harriet finally told Jill that she was uncomfortable with the situation, but she didn't really press the issue. Not surprisingly, nothing changed. As the year progressed, this problem continued to flare up until, finally, the roommates learned to speak more honestly. They survived their freshman year together, but both requested single rooms for sophomore year.

Points to Ponder

It may be one of the hardest things you do your freshman year, but you need to learn to speak up and speak the truth. Forget your fear about "rocking the boat" - you'll just become increasingly resentful if you don't tackle the issue. This does not mean you should go for the jugular, of course. Often a straightforward conversation will suffice, since many roommates simply don't realize that their actions are upsetting or that they've made erroneous assumptions about you and what you're OK with.

It's also important to remain aware and respectful of your roommate's moral comfort zone. It may be very different than yours, which for better or for worse is part of the college experience. This may sound painfully obvious, but it is surprisingly easy to forget. As Harriet pointed out in retrospect, the single most important lesson she learned from her roommate that year is that *"there were people who had completely different morals than me."*

The easiest way to deal with this tricky subject is to set up ground rules as early as possible. Wiggle the topic into those first late-night talkfests during Freshman Orientation. Find out what your roommate's feelings are about guys in the room, boyfriends (or girlfriends), public displays of affection and overnight guests - even if all the situations are hypothetical. Tell her your take on the matter. Roommates who didn't have serious problems with this issue usually had established some ground rules long before they were ever put to the test.

> **"**
> *I'm sorry to say that putting two strangers in a tiny space is just weird.*
> **"**
>
> JANE

EXPECT THE UNEXPECTED

You knew that college would be a whole new ball game. But did you ever think that your new roommate experience could be the emotional equivalent of squaring off against a tennis ball machine? You're poised and waiting, lightly tossing your racquet from hand to hand. Then, zing! From across the net the machine relentlessly spits out balls, sometimes straight at your head, sometimes to the far corner. If you don't stay on your toes, you're likely to do a face plant on the court.

While this metaphor may be a bit graphic, it's apt. Up until this point, you've doggedly labored up a steep trail strewn with SAT tutors, and honors classes, ballet lessons and summer internships to get to the summit. Now you've made it to the college of your choice – and, most likely, a roommate you didn't choose. So now what?

Here is what the tennis game of college-roommate-assignments served up to these students. See yourself in the following matches (so to speak)?

Coming from a sophisticated prep school in a major city, **Simone** expected a roommate from a similar background. Surprise, surprise. Emily came from a tiny, mid-western town and a graduating class of 10. In fact, with the exception of visiting the university, Emily had never traveled away from home. Other differences soon arose over religion, sleep patterns, cigarette smoking and even their age difference. Emily was two and a half years younger, having skipped several grades before high school.

"Emily was not like anyone I'd ever met," Simone recalled. *"She was very quiet with an innocence that is rare in my large city. And she was very young."*

Thanks to a family who emphasized the value of tolerance and acceptance, Simone was well prepared to deal with the initial stresses of her new living situation. As it turned out, Simone learned to focus better through Emily's example. Emily did not have dozens of friends visiting in the room at all hours, and was very bright and very studious. Throughout the year, the two roommates respected each other's space and learned about their differences.

For her sophomore year, Simone eventually moved in with five other girls,from her home state, but she is still friendly with Emily.

Jane and Franny never became friends and never reached the point of open hostility. The two roommates just never really meshed. There are certainly worse fates, but for a student like Jane, who eagerly looked forward to a stay-up-late-and-gossip kind of relationship with her roommate, this was crushingly disappointing.

Carefully manicured and quite chipper, Franny chewed gum and loved butterflies. Sure, the latter sounds innocuous, but butterfly posters dominated their room décor. Franny left the bathroom a-work-in-progress, with hair shavings scattered in the sink and red hair dye splattered on the shower floor. Her taste in music was tolerable. Barely. The problem was her insistence on hearing the same Tori Amos and Sarah McLaclan songs over and over and over. Adding insult upon injury, Franny used Jane's stereo for these concerts because her own was "temperamental."

Their academic schedules were also opposite. Franny was in a two-year bridge program, similar to high school. She attended classes all morning and participated in a scheduled study hall in the afternoon. On the weekends, Franny went home, preventing any bonding that may have been possible under normal circumstances. Jane, on the other hand, was in and out at all hours with irregularly scheduled classes and a haphazard nightlife.

Did these women ever establish good communication skills? Unfortunately no. After a semester of living together, they moved on. Game. Point. Match. Although it is not clear that anything they may have done differently would have saved this relationship, Jane's insight a year later was that if she had been more open, flexible and outspoken with Franny, their time together would have been more pleasant and rewarding.

Points to Ponder

Expect the unexpected. Remember the discovery rooms in a children's museum, where you insert a trembling hand into a gaping dark hole only to discover a soft rabbit on the other side? The fear can be paralyzing, but the pay-off is there for the taking (or petting).

Well, in meeting your roommate, it makes sense to expect the unexpected. As with any new relationship, it's important to remain open minded, curb early judgment, keep your sense of humor honed and ready, and be open to change.

Accentuate the positive. Unfortunately, we as humans have a tendency to jump straight to our fears and couch our expectations largely in the negative. Will I like her? She me? Will she be a nerd? Hate my favorite music? Can I tolerate hers? What if she's a neat freak? What if she steals my clothes or toothbrush? Gads, maybe she'll smell weird. This is the fast lane to unnecessary anxiety. While any or all of your con-

> **"**
> *... I leaned back and kissed my boyfriend. She ran for her Bible and read it for half an hour.*
> **"**
>
> *AYLA*

cerns may turn out to be founded, if you open your heart and mind when it comes to expectations, you might find the process of getting to know a possibly completely different person to be a pleasant experience, even a glorious one.

Be open to serendipity. She might be your instant soul sister. Or perhaps the two of you could qualify for a new "Odd Couple" sitcom. It may be a hard pill to swallow, but often these seemingly off-the-wall matches provide the most inspiring and educational friendships. So it may be hard, but be open to serendipity.

FILL OUT THE FORM TRUTHFULLY...AND PRAY THEY READ IT

A brutal fact is that each college and university has a different philosophy when it comes to roommate matching. Questionnaires can be surprisingly minimal. (The winner in this category goes to a large public university that sends out a form asking only: What time do you go to bed? Do you smoke?) Other institutions send out forms so detailed you might as well consider it an early start on writing your autobiography.

Regardless of how elaborate the roommate questionnaire, almost a third of the young women interviewed were incredulous at how seemingly off-kilter their roommate assignment was. Some wondered if anyone in their university's administration had ever actually read their questionnaires or had they recycled the forms immediately. Or was their pairing the result of deliberate social engineering, carefully designed by the university to broaden students' horizons?

Well, folks, sometimes you have no one to blame but yourself – as these women can attest.

Leila flat out lied on her form, saying that she didn't smoke to keep her parents from learning the truth. Not surprisingly, she ended up with a non-smoking roommate. Diana wasn't interviewed, but she must have been annoyed at Leila's self-serving deception.

On the flip side, **Jane** requested a smoking roommate on her form. But now she recalls, *"... I didn't know what a pack and a half of menthols a day meant."* What it meant was a relentless blue haze and the odor of menthol permeating clothes, hair, eyes and life. For Jane, a better solution might have been editorializing and indicating a light smoking habit rather than just checking a box, and hoping for the best. Another solution; request "non-smoking," then commit to smoking in authorized common areas or out of doors. Do this ONLY if you are a 100 percent sure you can keep this promise at all times. (See remarks on weather first!) Otherwise, you run the risk of becoming your roommate's nightmare.

Ann, whose small, elite university gave great thought to the assignment process, had these words of advice: *"Take the roommate selection form seriously and fill it out thoughtfully. You may think heavy metal music doesn't bother you. How about seven days a week?"* Ann personally had an excellent experience with her college-assigned roommate but she added this thought as well: *"Most college students enjoy their sophomore year more; they get to choose their roommates."*

Points to Ponder

Honesty is the best policy. Where have you heard that before? In this situation, it's imperative. Imagine a non-smoker trying to study in a room almost opaque from her roommates' exhales. Or try going to sleep at 10:00 p.m. when your roommate insists on flipping on the stereo at 1:00 a.m. when she settles in to study.

Be straight in your answers. Consider mailing the form without letting your parents see it so you don't feel that you have to lie. Misleading the housing committee just invites problems that could otherwise have been avoided.

And be prepared for surprises.

ODDS ARE, YOU'RE NOT IN KANSAS ANYMORE

Fortunes are contributed annually to support tolerance museums. Tolerance is taught in the home, in school and in church or temple. There's a reason so much time, effort and money are dedicated to this theme. And it becomes evident the moment you move into your college dorm.

Freshmen resident halls are typically total madhouses – and often a total blast to be in – because they bring together a wide variety of students from different backgrounds and cultures. Welcome to a Life Lesson, compliments of your university: Diversity gives you tools needed to deal successfully with post-school life. Theme dorms do exist on campuses, providing havens to the theater crowd or a computer-enthusiast enclave, but these are not always available to incoming freshmen.

> **❝**
> *You may think heavy metal music doesn't bother you. How about seven days a week?*
> **❞**
> ANN

The sheer overwhelming variety of humanity can make you run for cover under your duvet or keep you up talking all night in the laundry room with the fascinating oddballs from down the hall. Chances are at times it will make you want to do both. The key question becomes how you approach the situation.

The following roommate relationships had rocky starts based on preconceived ideas. Each turned out to have a happy ending. Though some students interviewed did not enjoy the happily-ever-after resolution, they still had differences which started as an impasse ended up changing in some way how they look at the world. The earlier tolerance is learned and practiced, the easier life is. Promise. After all, none of us gets to choose our bosses, our neighbors, or our bank tellers.

As an only child, **Lisa** enjoyed an extraordinarily quiet, and private, room at home. She abruptly discovered that she was ill prepared for the noise of college. There were no quiet hours, no peace, and little privacy. *"In the beginning, just sharing a room was a problem."* At first Lisa thought she and her roommate, Emily, would be incompatible. *"It was intimidating to talk to her. She came from an industrial area of a large city. We did not get along until second semester."* Almost imperceptibly, they both changed over the course of the year. As they shared experiences, they forgot about their differences and created a history of their own. Friendship followed. *"In the end [Emily] helped me to learn how to interact with different types of people. Now, in our sophomore year, we still room together. Emily and I are best friends. We chose to live with each other."*

Sara was initially shocked to walk into her new home away from home and see Khadija, her Saudi Arabian roommate, who along with her mother were swathed head to toe in identical black Muslim veils. As they got to know each other, Sara and Khadija discovered that they shared the same sense of humor and quirky sleep habits (lots of naps). *"We are perfectly happy living in a mess."* Any problems created by their totally different backgrounds seemed irrelevant. *"I grew,"* Sara said, who felt that she became more open to different people thanks to Khadija. The two women remain close friends to this day.

Of course, this somewhat alien creature now known as your roommate may turn out to be precisely what you need. Somewhere during her last two years in high school, **Kate** realized she was ready for change. It was time to leave her urban high school, leave her friends – some of whom she had known since kindergarten – and create a home away from her family home. *"It was some sort of an identity crisis."* Without sacrificing her good school performance, Kate desperately wanted to break out of her mold and go far, far away to a college where she could be start fresh. And be a little bit wild. Kate's roommate, Marcy, ended up being a great match precisely because she helped Kate take a walk on her wilder side. *"Marcy is the wild child I'd never been, but not obnoxiously so."* Under Kate's influence, Marcy calmed down a bit. They were role models for each other, and became fast friends.

Points to Ponder

It's very possible that you will be paired with a roommate who under other circumstances you might never take the time to cross the quad and chat with. In larger universities, you can almost count on this. So, there are many things to keep in mind here:

1. You are not defined by your roommate.

2. Depending on your academic schedule, extracurricular activities, and social life, you might not have that much contact with her.

3. Okay, so you have little in common. And there are times when it seems none of your efforts communicate your true feelings. Or she simply doesn't understand you. You come from different cultures, have widely disparate sleeping habits, or opposing ideas about life. Most institutions of higher learning would agree that education does not stop in the classroom. There is much to be learned from rooming with someone. Especially in a small room.

4. Post-college life should come with a 100%, money-back guarantee that situations will be far more complicated and difficult than a completely alien roommate. So try to think of an imperfect roommate as training wheels for your future. (We know, we know, you're tired of hearing this one, but try to keep your eye on the prize.)

5. Great payoffs can come from tolerance.

REAL LIVE SOCIAL EXPERIMENTS

Roommate pairings can feel like cruel jokes or bad sitcom scripts concocted by a bored, under-appreciated college committee in charge of mixing and matching their way through freshman dorms. How else do you explain the fact that you

" We did not get along until second semester. "

LISA

and your from-another-galaxy roommate were thrown together? This is probably closer to the truth. Sometimes the pairings are accidental. Sometimes they are divinely inspired. And sometimes it is calculated social engineering, guided by college administrators who pair people with disparate backgrounds and personalities in the hopes of enriching social awareness and expanding your horizons.

Sometimes this experiment survives and thrives, but after all, these are mere mortals. Sometimes the social engineering never really flies. It's up to you to rise to meet the challenge (and yes, it can be a major challenge), or at the very least to learn how to best manage the situation.

For **Abby** and Jessica dissonance started on day one with the unfortunately revealed fact that Jessica was a scholarship student. On move-in day, the university (with shocking insensitivity) sent a package of books, supplies and a distinctive version of a required desk lamp to all scholarship students. The lamp might as well have been a neon sign flashing 'scholarship kid here.' Jessica never had the chance or choice to tell Abby at her discretion that she was on a scholarship. Abby didn't care that Jessica was on scholarship, but this bit of information, shared in this manner, left both girls feeling awkward.

    From Abby's point of view (rightly or wrongly), Jessica became defensive and shut Abby out when the scholarship lamp became obvious. Moreover, Abby – whose parents were struggling to pay full fare tuition – felt vaguely irritated. Unfortunately, neither girl felt comfortable discussing the issue. Both beat emotional retreats, undermining their relationship before it ever got off the ground.

    There were other problems. Abby recalls being very specific on her housing form, reporting that she went to bed at 3:00 a.m. Jessica crawled into the sack by 9:00 p.m. In addition, the women spent no time together on the weekend since Jessica's parents – who lived only a couple of hours away – visited, while Abby hopped into the city for entertainment. Not that they would have necessarily have hung out together on a Sunday, since they had absolutely nothing in common.

    "We were not compatible," Abby said. *"Even though I took the time over the summer to fill out a questionnaire about the kind of roommate I would like, the roommate I was assigned had nothing in common with the characteristics I put down."*

    After three or four months of living together, the women had a massive fight and Jessica moved out. At least that helped Abby's situation.

Like most freshmen, **Alexandra** struggled with the transition to college life. But her experience was *nothing* compared to what her roommate, Ana, was experiencing: "My roommate couldn't have been more different. *"Ana was a Bosnian refugee and me, a girl from* *[a large American city]. I think that says it all."*

This was such an extreme pairing that it created a dynamic of its own (thereby fulfilling the deepest fantasy of every administrator who ever tackled the task of designating roommates). Alexandra saw her own life in a new perspective, and was enormously impressed with Ana's strength and resolve. Their everyday exchanges were enlightening and engaging. Alexandra felt that this socially engineered roommate provided the thread of sanity with which to redouble her commitment to stay at the university.

While her experience was positive, Alexandra had strong advice for freshmen. *"I recommend having a roommate freshman year, definitely - as far as transition goes, but after that, having a single is the way to go."*

Points to Ponder

Relax, you may not be paranoid after all. You may be correct in suspecting that you were tapped to be a Chosen One when it came to the politically correct, socially engineered roommate game.

Consider the alternate. It may be a rocky road to hell, but really worth it to make the enormous effort that may be needed to make your dorm room a happy home for the year. After all, didn't you come to college to get your mind blown?

So what's the best approach in these situations? Simple: communicate, be straightforward, be assertive, and be polite. Remember, friendships take time to take root.

Who goes first? Should you go out on a limb and make the effort when she doesn't? Why not give it a try? You could turn the situation around, and it's much more pleasant to come home to a relaxed, friendly environment than to one in which you feel you're dodging land mines. Also, changing roommates usually is a dauntingly difficult process, and who's to say that your next assignment would be any better?

Do you absolutely, positively have to get out? You know what to do. Go up the chain of command starting with the Resident Advisor in your hall. Rationally explain why things just aren't working. Keep on top of the process and paper work. And good luck.

> **"**
> ***We are
> perfectly
> happy
> living
> in a mess.***
> **"**
>
> *SARA*

DON'T ROMANTICIZE

Thanks to Hollywood or your own flights of imagination while pouring over college catalogues, odds are you have preconceived expectations about your roommate experience before you ever step foot on your campus. Go on, admit it. Good or bad, the images are there. Preparation is always good, but getting too locked into your own expectations can make for a wretched prison once you finally meet your roommate and get to know each other.

Reality of course is infinite in its variety, but for the most part, all roommate scenarios can be boiled down into five basic categories:

1. **Insta-Friend.** Bond immediately, develop mutual love and understanding, become lifelong friends.

2. **Bobsled Run.** Great compassion and enthusiasm at first, but it's all downhill from there. As the weeks progress the situation grows suffocating.

3. **No-hope Odd Couple.** Opposites from the start with no reprieve; either you demonstrate super tolerance or you switch roommates.

4. **Mistaken Identity.** Hatred on sight, but things pick up as you get to know each other. Communication and tolerance emerge, then evolve into a supportive and enriching friendship.

5. **Benchwarmer.** You're there, you're not going anywhere, but there is never any real connection. Wait out your time in peace and quiet, and find friends elsewhere.

Your job is to make the most of whatever cards are dealt to you. See how the various pairings below played out.

For better or for worse, **Jeni** dreamed of an all-American collegiate experience, and in part chose her university for the all-American atmosphere: football, pep rallies, bonfires and late night gabfests with a similarly minded roommate. The discovery that her new roommate was from Indonesia caused quite a surprise. Jeni felt that ***"someone from Kentucky was foreign enough."*** Jeni's dreams evaporated when she found that her roommate had never even heard of football. That long-cherished image of her first year in college died slowly. Then, looking around and seeing much worse roomie situations, Jeni decided to stick it out for the rest of the year. The two never exactly became buddies, but they established a livable environment. Jeni learned tolerance. Her roommate learned football. *"My roommate and I are not friends, but we respect each other's space and can get along. I am definitely not thrilled with her, but it worked out OK."*

Even after a year, **Lola** wondered how she was selected to room with Martha. Squinting at the walls, she guessed they each had an interest in art, but that was generous, according to Lola. On the roommate notification form, Martha had appeared exotic. She lived in Asia for 10 years and had conducted an impressive research project the summer before college. Lola fantasized about the trips to this faraway land that she and her new best friend would take.

Reality hit. As usual, it was harsh.

Martha slept an extraordinary amount of time – she slept in when Lola left in the morning, took catnaps during the day, and still managed to crash early at night. She was also sick a lot, with a disgustingly resonate cough ("gak gak gak"). It got to the point that, although Lola liked to study in her room, she didn't feel it was a pleasant or even healthy environment in which to hang out. To round off the package, Martha had a pushy personality, too assertive for Lola's taste, and was not particularly clean. Sheets and laundry seemed to be vying for the *Guinness Book of World Records"* entry regarding longest time between washes.

It got to the point that Lola's friends refused to hang out in her room if her roommate was there. Lola went to her dean for a room change. Despite Lola getting increasingly vocal, no action was taken, so she just had to tough out the year. She settled into a six-room suite sans Martha for sophomore year. Though the situation was far better than her previous year, Lola didn't find that idyllic roommate she had originally envisioned. She now thoughtfully wonders, *"Why, indeed, are there roommates in college? Is it really a necessary part of the transition?"*

Then there's **Jane** again. After getting out of her unhappy situation with Franny, Jane moved in with best-friend-since-kindergarten Brittany for the second semester.

Hope: Better than Insta-friend.

Reality: Jane and Brittany fought ferociously, turning their room into a tense battleground. Both were in relationships and got caught up in the snippy whirlwind of gossiping about the other's whereabouts and activities. They were way too involved in each other's lives. Miraculously, they remained friends, but lived apart the following year.

> **"**
> *...someone from Kentucky was foreign enough.*
> **"**
> JENI

Points to Ponder

Romantics can get hurt. This may sound harsh, but perhaps it's a *good* idea not to have the highest expectations about residence hall life. This doesn't mean you should become a queen cynic or embrace negativity, but just acknowledge that the situation may be out of your control – just as the quality of your dorm food will be. But what can you do?

What is the bottom line? Your room is just a place to hang your clothes and rest your head. If you discover your roommate is very cool and fun, and you have a blast hanging out together, then lucky you. If the situation is middle of the road, lucky you. But if it's intolerable, well, tomorrow *is* another day. Between your Resident Advisor (R.A.) and the Campus Housing Office, you can request a change. Even if that doesn't work, the summer will arrive sooner than you think. A bum roommate really is no big deal in the grand scheme of things. Honest.

Also, don't forget that sometimes it's y-o-u, dear. We all know you're special, but roommate life is different. Maybe you're an active part of the problem. If you realize that, you stand a good chance of improving the situation. Your best tool will be a healthy, if not overdeveloped dose of humor. Perfection is overrated, anyway. And remember, it's only nine months and counting.

GO FORTH AND MAKE FRIENDS

Your future roommate is a single person. Your residence hall mates may be a couple hundred more, and your classmates may be a couple thousand more. Regardless of what stage of nirvana you and your roommate reside in (or don't), take advantage of your uniquely social setting! In life, you'll never again be surrounded by so many like-minded, bright, and interesting people who are just about your age. Classes, the cafeteria, the laundry room (time honored meeting ground), rehearsals for a theater production, sports, varsity or intramural, down the hall or across the campus. It's a downright bonanza out there. Get going!

Amber went in blind to her housing situation since her university provided no advanced questionnaire and she had absolutely no advance info on her roomie. To her great surprise, she and her roommate got along well from the start. It wasn't the case for everyone in her residence hall. *"I know people in my hall had problems with their roommates, but they were able to switch."*
Their residence hall was in a far corner of campus, and Amber found herself rela-

tively isolated from the drama department activities that she found most rewarding. So while Amber made her closest friends in the activities provided by drama, the hall's location forced Amber and most of her dorm mates to bond and form friendships readily. In a sense, they really only had each other. *"We learned together how to really deal with sharing our entire lives with another being, respecting each other completely."*

One Last Point to Ponder

Dorm friends will be central in your new life, and are certainly convenient. Still, residence hall life is only part of the overall college package. Be open to all the opportunities that abound. Don't limit yourself. Your friends and you yourself will be more interesting for it.

QUICK TAKES

Be careful what you wish for. It can happen that your roommate matches you so perfectly that you seem like each other's clones. Sharing similar philosophies – be they religious, financial, educational, social, or economical – can offer instant, unbelievable friendships. Unhappily, the result can sometimes be an overbearing, possessive relationship that scares off the outside world. Not to overly concern yourself with what appears to be a perfect match, but be aware that things can turn sour.

   Impressed that her college wanted her to fill out a three-pageroommate selection document, **Harriet** was amazed and delighted at the school's choice of roommate for her. She and Jill were perfectly matched. Too perfectly. *"We became each other's parents. Tell me where you are, when you're coming home…"* The two ended up nagging each other, which made for a lo-o-o-ng year. It wasn't until towards the end of the year that they both learned to speak up and set more appropriate guidelines.

Your roomie could be your lifeline. Plenty of roommates reported a sense of mutual concern and caring. What wonderful serendipity.

   Leila and Diana felt instantly compatible. Theirs was the relationship about which Judy Bloom books were written. *"In two to three weeks we were ultra close, and had a friendship like sisters."* (*She must not have had a sister!*) Both had boyfriends, neither pledged a sorority; they had an

> **Why, indeed, are there roommates in college? Is it really a necessary part of the transition?**
>
> LOLA

open-closet policy, followed the same general sleep patterns, and shared one computer. Alas, Leila disliked her chosen university with an industrial-strength ferocity. It was too big, too haughty, too politically correct, too hypocritical. While the unfriendly winds raged outside – her boyfriend a continent away and her family not responsive enough for her satisfaction – Diana became an important and safe relationship for Leila. Feelings of loneliness and the fearsome prospect of informing her parents that she wanted to leave were consuming pastimes. Ultimately, Leila did leave this university and moved to another larger, better-for-Leila option. Diana remained at the original school, but the two women remained very close. They were lucky to be so compatible. Leila was also lucky for her roommate's loyalty during a stressful time. They made the most of what the matching system provided.

Bid a fond farewell to privacy. Whether you were an only child, enjoyed your own bedroom at home, or shared a bathroom with siblings, living with a roommate in college is just plain different. Family members grow to work around each other's quirkiness and habits. Roommates are thrown together with no formality, just the rather wobbly hope that you two will work things out.

 Jane dreaded going to her dorm room. *"It sucks living in a strange place, in a big city and you dread going home. I wanted to be alone but it was just not possible. Maybe I was spoiled growing up. I used to enjoy a lot of space. There were four years when I shared a bathroom with my brother, but he was respectful of my space."*

 Perhaps it's smart to start playing what-if games long before you unpack your first suitcase at the dorm. You may sleep in Dr. Dentons, while your roommate sleeps in the raw. You may love chatting while you fall asleep, while your roommate has a Japanese screen erected to give her more privacy. Personal space issues can arise over phone calls, writing e-mails, or even listening to music. Potential pitfalls are everywhere unless you think and plan a bit.

> **"**
> *In two to three weeks we were ultra close, and had a friendship like sisters.*
> **"**
>
> LEILA

The inescapable Golden Rule. Hey, that's my sweater you're wearing! Where are my new CDs? Did you borrow my history notes? Can't you ever fall asleep without listening to Kenny G?

 That good ol' Golden Rule: Do unto others as you would have others do unto you. It's obvious, but effective. The most successful relationships, be they platonic or romantic, are grounded in good communications, understanding and respect. Sometimes it's just so hard to remember that, however, when you discover that your roommate ate your last, long-hoarded Girl Scout cookies or stained your favorite skirt.

In a Midwestern college town, **Libby's** particular last straw was her discovery that her roommate Anika surreptitiously wore her clothing to class and events, only to fold and return the articles to Libby's drawer as if nothing had happened. The women had never agreed to share clothes. They finally got into a fight – over this and other factors – and Libby moved out.

While some of these stories don't have a happy ending, the upside is obviously there. Relating well to others is a second career no matter what your path in life. Advice. Do your best here!

9-1-1. Every college has them.

R.A.s or resident advisors are comprised of upperclassmen (sometimes sophomores), trained by the university to understand policies, procedures, rules, and how to handle emergencies. They can help with advice on certain physical problems. Most importantly they have been given insights into matters of the heart, be it homesickness or a new boyfriend or lack of friendships or too much pressure. R.A.s have also been down the road you are traveling, very recently. In fact they could be mommy-in-a-pinch, though they might be guys. Use 'em.

Problems bigger than all that, or you don't want to spill tears right where you live? It is almost assured that you will find a Counseling Center, with a staff of professionals, on your campus. They too can help with the adjustment issues you are facing. The name might be different, but the function remains the same. They have heard it all and it's a sure bet that they can help. Most of the young women interviewed mentioned their counseling center. Everyone thought it was good advice. But no one ever did it. Ever. Perhaps you'll be a first.

• •

ROOMIE SOLUTIONS

Here's the microwave popcorn version of the major points made in this chapter. Keep them for ready reference once the honeymoon period is over.

Speak up. Speak the truth. Many of the problems are caused by erroneous assumptions. She thinks you're a morning person. You're not. She thinks you like to lend your clothes. You don't. She thinks you don't mind if her boyfriend sleeps over. No way! Get the picture?

Take it seriously. Having shared a room with a sibling or summers at sleep-away camp does *not* guarantee success with a college roommate. This is a whole new ball game, without the convenient parent referees. And a couple weeks at camp only gives you a taste of the harsh reality of nine months of cohabitation.

Fill out the form honestly. And carefully. You may think you can live with any kind of music, but what if you are the only one willing to live with the person who likes heavy metal? How quickly will it drive you nuts if it's on every freaking day?

Don't romanticize. Despite your best efforts to finesse the roommate questionnaire and cheery hopes about your new best friend, you still might get a no-go match up. Make the most of it. You're here to learn, right? 'Wait and see' may be the second key to this point. She seems like a great match, then, whoops. Where did that oboe come from? Perhaps it would be easier if you hadn't been such a good sport all along. Being cooperative is good; being a push-over bad. And honesty is pretty much required.

The Golden Rule. Don't like to lend clothes? Don't borrow. Don't like to be awakened by loud music? Maybe she doesn't like to go to sleep with it playing in the background. If you think something may be intrusive, ask. Think about your life from her perspective, and consider if your habits invade any of her senses or sensibilities. And watch the body language as well as listen to the words. "Let me think about it" usually means "no."

Be open: You and your roommate will change. Once in college, freed from the rituals and rules of home, you're going to change – a lot. Bedtime, for example, is going to shift dramatically, as will other habits and even belief systems.

Try to find something in common. Come on. You're smart. Figure out what she likes. Determine when she'll be around and try to hang out with her in the room. But, is this all your responsibility? No way! But if neither of you reaches out, then what?

Make friends outside your suite/hall/dorm. Living life under the microscope that is a residence hall is limiting. Get out and about. Get involved with interest groups, sports, and study groups (help the ol' GPA). Remember, these are some of the things you did (and maybe even enjoyed) to get into college in the first place.

Perhaps the counseling center can help. Think of this. The other students are new too, muddling through the best they can. Some are openly scared; some put on a brave front. The counseling service, by whatever name it is called on your particular campus, has seen it all. Everything. Things you can't even think of. The counselors probably spend the better part of September and October enjoying the vistas from their office windows, or putting together under-attended discussion groups designed to support the major transition you're going through. If you feel that you need a voice of reason or support, give the counseling office a try. They know what they're doing, and even better, services are generally free to enrolled students.

Can we at least be civil? If things work out well, congratulations. But if they don't, the worst that can happen is that you want a new roomie or want to be alone. Find out your college's policy and see if you can get a satisfactory resolution. If that fails – and it very well might – consider openness as another way to turn this situation into a livable one. Explain exactly what the problem is, and if possible, why. Use "I messages." Example: "I have a problem with daily oboe practice." Versus: "Your oboe depresses and annoys me every morning."

Enjoy the social engineering. What else can you do? Colleges (at least some) intentionally pair students from divergent backgrounds to help make them grow, gain perspective, and demonstrate common values. Sometimes it even works. Regardless, you may as well sit back and try to enjoy the ride to the best of your abilities. Frequently, there is nothing you can change – but there is always next year.

• •

Where's the Psychic Friends Network When You Really Need It?

No matter who you are and how extroverted you may be, when it comes to making new friends every freshman fears the worst. Insecurities that may have been conquered years ago or even last week are sure to crop up, and nightmares of junior high school agony may revisit. Sorry.

There's no downplaying these fears. Everyone is plagued by them. But think about it ... *everyone* has the same concerns of friend-less-ness. You, my friend, are far from alone. And while some freshmen may fall into the insecurity-born trap of closing themselves off emotionally, most won't. The first year of college arguably is the easiest period in one's entire life to make friends because so many people are simultaneously open to new experiences and relationships. Many times it is here, more so than in high school even, where most lifelong friendships are forged.

And when friendships develop, it makes all the difference in the college experience. For the young women interviewed, everything clicked into place. So the real question on the table is how to make friends? What's the best approach, what will ease the process and what are the pitfalls along the way?

As **Ann** summarized: *"You only have these four years when you'll be living 24 hours/7 days a week with your friends. If you work all the time, you'll miss out on the opportunity to meet really cool people and have really memorable experiences. It's important to* *balance school work and your social life."*

First, a quick recap of the basics: In college you are thrown together with a diverse group of people, each coming from radically different backgrounds and each bearing dramatically different goals. On the other hand, just being admitted to and selecting the same college means that you automatically have some common ground. The majority of entering students start college without a best high school friend or sibling at their side. That puts you all in the same boat.

Take a look at how these young women fared with friends as they proceeded on their college paths and what they learned along the way. More importantly, keep an eye out for the most common theme: Be friendly and open, and the friendship karma will come back at you.

OLD, NEW, SAME, DIFFERENT? ARGH!

This may or may not be good news. If you were more than ready to shrug the bonds and labels of high school, you're sprung! However, if you loved every minute of high school, well, you're sprung anyway. Whether you like it or not, it's time to move forward. This means leaving behind the friends who know you inside and out, the wench who still taunts you about the time you threw up in sixth grade, your soul-mate confidante, the clique you never wanted to be considered a part of or the clique you dreamed about, and the numbers game (the more friends you have, the more popular). As you can see, this is truly a mixed blessing, but at the very least everyone starts with a clean slate.

With this fresh start and the chance to explore new avenues both in college and within your psyche, the next question is what kind of friends do you want? What kind will turn out to be the best? It's so easy to find and quickly bond with people much like your old friends. And having some such friends at college is a wonderful security blanket. But it's worth considering looking beyond that. Open your horizons and your eyes, think outside your personal box, and strive to make friends for the new woman who you are becoming.

The actual process of making friends appears to fall along the same general path, whether at big, diverse universities or small, more homogeneous colleges. It starts with being receptive, observing the scene, acting and reacting, and surviving the tad bit of uneasiness that everyone feels when going out on a personal limb. Here are the stories.

Anne B. felt that for her, *"At college there were many NICE people, but they didn't seem* *to know my history. My high school friends had seen me in so many situations. In college it was tiring to create a good impression, to be 'on stage.' Ironically I was starting in college with a clean slate, and this was a main goal from high school, but this was also the problem."*

Anne's first stabs at forging friendships were cautious. She engaged in long talks with new people, established a routine, found time to sleep, bottled some loneliness. What held everything together was confidence that she would eventually find the friendships she wanted. *"I know there are good people at my school who will be good friends."* It's just that it seemed to be taking awhile, and nostalgia would intrude. *"[Sometimes I would see] something that would make me think an old friend should see [it, too or they] would love [it as well], whatever it was."*

Anne, who originally was unsure how and where to look for friendships, eventually came to these conclusions. *"Make sure you know who you are and don't try to change to find friends. Take advantage of friends, especially the weird and kookie ones. They have the most to share. It's not how many friends you have but the quality of the friendships you do make. Life doesn't revolve around classes and work. Yes, you should work hard, and worry about the future, but don't forget to have FUN."*

Sara slowly realized that she had become less concerned with the image of her friends. *"'The Popular Crowd' and 'The Beautiful People' became meaningless. 'Funny' has become a priority, not necessarily 'stylish.'"* This was a major breakthrough for Sara, who used good looks as an entrance requirement for friendship in her life. As her requirement for appearances dropped, she realized that she now has diverse friends, different from those in high school and different from each other. Slowly she found friends. She loved talking with them in small groups at the many venues on campus. Life became a series of fluid social vignettes; a snack in the cafeteria moving on to new group forming on a bench in the quad then scattering and reorganizing on the steps. In addition to the true-blue friends, she also gained a coterie of casual friends with whom she had a total blast.

Sam's new group of friends was fairly homogeneous, yet very different from the big-city, ultra-sophisticated friends she'd known back home. Her new friends appealed to a calmer side of Sam. No weekly therapy appointments, no families suffering through divorce. These friends appeared more sheltered. So great were the contrasts that Sam sometimes found herself thinking that her life was *"a joke and theirs the perfect world."* She liked the difference. Sam

> **"**
> *In college it was tiring to create a good impression, to be 'on stage.'*
> **"**
> ANNE B.

thought that her new friends may perceive her as the ***"feminist, funky chick by comparison."*** (Not to belabor the obvious, but since these are friends they obviously share the same values and interests deep down.) She made her friends slowly and thoughtfully, and her social life blossomed. Her roommate became one of her closest friends. Sam felt at home.

Lauren looked around and worried that *"everyone would be dorky computer nerds."* She initially hung out on the periphery of groups before finally jumping in fully. The maybe-nerds turned out to be well-rounded, smart, social and fun. It took three weeks – which felt like a mini-eternity, but was really just a blip – and then Lauren felt settled in. She was part of the college swing, and at home.

One of the biggest changes for **Meredith** came from the realization her college friends came from different economic backgrounds. ***"I suddenly have a lot of friends whose families aren't as well off as mine which was a shock. Not bad, just different."***

Points to Ponder

No one knows you. This might be a good thing. You can forget the immature things you regret from high school years, or move past the stupid classification that former classmates dismissed you as. You begin with a fresh slate.

You could assume this might be the perfect opportunity to re-create yourself. After all, this is the right and privilege that the freedom of college confers upon you. Just make sure that you stay true to yourself, whatever changes you make. Remember, these are folks who might be in your life for the rest of your life on a personal and professional basis. Don't you want to present the real you? Besides, the alternative is exhausting.

Throw whatever social rulebook you may have followed out the window. There aren't rules regarding who can become your friends, and folks are much less judgmental in college when it comes to you and your friends. Different isn't bad; it can be illuminating. This is obvious, but friends come in all packages. Try on a variety for size, so to speak. You never know who might be the perfect fit!

Be friendly. Oh, so simple but that's really what works. All the freshmen are new. Sometimes when people look and act intimidating, they are simply frightened or nervous. Why not be the first to make a move? You really have nothing to lose.

THE TORTOISE AND THE HARE

Friendship is like making great soup; speed is not the issue. While there can be instant bonds, friendship often just takes time. Time to assemble, time to simmer and savor and time to enjoy.

For somewhere near two months, **Karen** lived in a room designated as a single with another student; Karen being "the temporary roommate." While she found her unwitting hostess lovely, Karen characterized the uncertainty and unsettled-ness as *"frightening."* Then she discovered that incoming freshmen are generally assigned to single rooms. Aspirations, real or imagined, that the perfect roommate would be also be a wonderful, close friend were simply not going to happen.

Luckily, during this time, Karen met Korean-born Aimee. Finding lots in common philosophically, they became fast friends. The diverse and interesting portion of her college dream was beginning to fall into place.

But things were still rocky. Having come from a close knit family, where meal time was a fond memory, she initially feared she wouldn't *"have anyone to go out with, like to dinner."* For Karen, a turning point was *"when I started to expect who I was going to eat with and make plans with."*

Finally, a breakthrough. After Thanksgiving Karen moved into her very own single room, serendipitously located in the same building as Aimee, just one floor below. This made it more convenient for Karen to see her friend and also find herself in the middle of a joyful group that Aimee had already formed. While Karen still felt lonely after socializing and then returning to her single room, the incidents were fewer and less frequent. *"At times, there are moments when I feel so good and so lucky."* Also a level of comfort emerged for Karen when she had a chance to personalize her room. Up went the curtain. Rows of pictures attached with haphazard pushpins and squishy old pillows. There. Done. Slowly, it all came together.

Frightened and quite lonely, **Leslie** found it difficult leaving the friends she had had in high school. She turned to the telephone and friends at their own colleges for comfort and help. *"I don't live in a very social, active hallway and it took a long time to meet people. I was frightened before I had formed any group of friends."* Finally, she met Jon, who was looking for help in math. That was the beginning of Leslie's social interaction. *"I was able to really attach to a friend*

> **" Make sure you know who you are and don't try to change to find friends. "**
>
> ANNE B.

and began to be able to count on not being left alone on weekends or at mealtimes."
Leslie also took the slow road, and it worked for her.

Simone, in retrospect, saw she had a mission. She sought people who were *"really smart, really social and fascinating, all rolled into one."* In looking for these new friends, she discovered that they, too, had had difficulty meeting girlfriends and that very problem became the foundation for the great friendships they soon enjoyed. She characterized her friends today as *"urban, attractive, outspoken, and ambitious."*

    "When I met those people with whom I am friends now and I get that spark, that connection, and I realize this is someone who is on the same wavelength. I still get that connection once in a while when I meet new friends. It's always exciting, but now I have the security of knowing that I already have friends like that at school."
Simone gave herself the gift of introspection, and her life, and the friendships fell into place.

Ann made three, maybe four good friends in a short amount of time. This made her feel good. *"They know everything about me. I am closer to them than to some high school friends I have known for 10 years."* For Ann, it was a speedy road to friendships and it worked for her.

Points to Ponder

Friendship is a process, and it can take time. Jumping into a deep friendship so fast that you barely have time to get to know the person can end up being as painful as jumping into an amorous relationship too fast. Moving more slowly might just be what leads to a lifelong friendship. Be prepared for the slow blossoming, keep the doors open, and enjoy the process. Or perhaps you meet a soul mate on Friday and you both know it by Saturday. Regardless, remember to evaluate as you go along. Friendships are a game of quality, not quantity.

You're not alone. Everyone else is new, just like you. They all had friends back home, and they are looking for new compadres. Go out and about with an open mind, even if it feels scary, and you are sure to find kindred souls.

Soup's on! For almost every single woman interviewed, mealtimes emerged as a central activity in the friend-finding and friend-making process. There are a ton of tactics here, depending on your comfort level. Invite someone to go down to breakfast/lunch/dinner with you. Make yourself available for an invite. Plunk your plate or tray down next to a friendly looking group of suspects. Almost anything goes here. What absolutely *won't* work is staying in your room with the door half shut, locked in a solitary activity like reading a book or cruising the Web.

BIRDS OF A FEATHER

All good clichés have a core of truth in them. Hence their annoying durability. So instead of just rolling your eyes when some well-meaning advice giver chimes "birds of a feather flock together," think about it. Learn it. Live it. Love it.

As you make your new life at college, get involved in activities on campus, off campus, in the residential halls or in the community. These could be interests that you've carried with you from high school, or something entirely brand new. All are great venues for finding friends of like interests and mindset.

Just a quick reminder, however. Get involved in what *you* want, not what the really hot guy across the hall is into. (And this temptation happens.) While it may have strategic value, you'll probably not enjoy yourself in the long run as much as spending your precious free time on what makes you truly happy. Which makes you a better friend, a happier person, and probably more intriguing to that hot guy from across the hall, anyway.

Sophie started her college search wanting a great drama program in a great university. She got it, which partly smoothed her transition to college and gave her the friendships she needed. A turning point for her was *"being accepted into the theatre community. The extracurricular activities are the icing on the cake! They make my college experience so great."*

Avoiding the easy pitfall of being too insular, Sophie also found great friends in her residence hall. At first she saw herself living in an *"environment of strangers."* Now these strangers are friends to call on. Yes, there can be intense, stressful disagreements. *"Sometimes new friends aren't close enough to confide their deepest secrets."* But in all, school grew comfortable to Sophie. Her happiest times were *"out with my friends, laughing with them."* Gradually she was pleasantly surprised *"that I began to feel as if my college were my home."*

Amber found great joy and opened herself up to friendships by creating events. She absolutely loved being a disc jockey at the wrap party for the fall play, helping a friend throw a

> **"**
> **I don't live
> in a
> very social,
> active
> hallway
> and
> it took
> a long time
> to
> meet people.
> "**
> LESLIE

hall barbecue. Spontaneous events were fun too: her personal favorite memory is *"a dorm-wide pillow fight."* By throwing herself in the thick of things, Amber found herself making good friends.

Points to Ponder

What rocks your soul? Think about what activities you're interested, and what kind of people you most want to be with. Be honest with yourself, and be honest about yourself. As said elsewhere in this book, college is an amazing time to expand your boundaries, so it's actually worth your time to really ponder what you want.

Just do it. So you've thought about what you want ... now do it. Be forthright and direct about joining activities. People tend to be more welcoming than we give than credit for. Be open to having different circles of friends, and let each one develop at their own pace.

Missing your ol' Saturday night poker game. Or bowling league, or hiking club, or whatever? What ever it is, if it doesn't already exist on campus, create a new club, organization or group. Solicit members (all potential friends), and get the group and your social life off the ground. If you build it, they will come!

MI PROBLEMA ES SU PROBLEMA AND VICE VERSA

With friendships can come stress. That's the risk of opening your heart and life to someone. A suitemate's grade crisis or your best friend's boyfriend-heartache can temporarily take over your entire life as you let them talk through it till 3:00 a.m., or cry on your shoulder for days on end. Be prepared. Be patient, as long as it doesn't become too serious a burden. And be confident in knowing that you've earned the right to run down the hall for a little reciprocal TLC.

> **"**
> *I'll remember my friendships, not my hours studying when I leave college.*
> **"**
> ANN

Ann realized the stresses of friendship were part of the learning experience. *"There was lots of opportunity to experience lots of emotion; goodness and badness. This is a good thing. I don't regret the stress or frustrations with both academics and friends. I figure I'll learn from it all."* As a sophomore, she now reflects: *"Living with 200 people all your age is a fantastic experience, but you are bound to fall into con-*

flicts. This year I have definitely stayed up late trying to sort friendship problems out - all of it worth it. I'll remember my friendships, not my hours studying when I leave college."

For **Scarlett,** new friendships had some understandably frightening aspects, like *"hearing and seeing friends' problems; and having the knowledge [those problems] could happen to you."* She also felt that some times were difficult and lonely, even though surrounded by friends. During rough patches such as finals, Scarlett didn't feel comfortable looking for some friendly support *"when I had a problem and technically could have gone to a friend."*

Points to Ponder

Friends and problems go hand-in-hand. Venting and advice are key elements to most friendships. Hopefully it is a two-way street. As long as it all stays in proportion, fine.

If you find yourself overwhelmed with someone else's problems, get help. You want to be a good friend, and you probably are. But sometimes the problems are just too big for a mere mortal, or sometimes someone else's stress may be taking over your life. This is probably not helpful either to you or to your friend. It's time to get help for the friend or for you if you're feeling truly overwhelmed. Try the hall advisor, the folks in the counseling service, or maybe your parents. There's just no need to go it alone.

INSIGHT POTPOURRI

The following is a collection of ideas about friendship from a number of the interviewees. These are personal tales of what made friendships new, special or possible. See what you can identify with, or what leaves you shaking your head.

The Little Things. Sometimes the best friends are those with whom you can make an utter fool of yourself without fear.

    Ann enjoyed the silly times *"…playing in the snow, ice skating, Christmas caroling, making movies. I especially loved dancing to 'Jesus Christ Superstar' and videotaping it. Comfortable times are nice too. In my room, sitting on my bed with a cup of tea, talking to my roommate about my day."*

    Holden's favorite early memories were of *"girls' night*

> **"**
> *In the beginning, it seemed to me that everyone knew someone and I didn't.*
> **"**
>
> LISA

in the dorm, dancing on the beds and drinking my personal favorite, Snapple and vodka." She loved the hysterical laughter, and just a plain old good time.

The Guy Quotient. They often have completely different viewpoints or advice, expose you to a new world of activities, teach you greater understanding of the opposite sex (very helpful when dealing with dates), and they don't borrow your mascara!

Meredith remarked that *"in high school, all my close friends with the exception of four or five were female. At college, it's the opposite."* Other young women reported similar ratios.

Joanne said that *"it's great having immediate access to guys. It's a great stress reliever."* At Joanne's college, room assignments are boy-girl-boy-girl along the same hall, and the bathrooms are co-ed, which was a bit more exposure than she had expected. But it made it easy to make friends of both genders, and she found guys to be looser, friendlier and generally more open.

For **Charlotte,** who attended a small campus, it was easy to be *"friends with guys given the closer quarters."* She also found it harder to have romantic relationships with them because of this proximity. Seeing last night's date at the community breakfast table was more intimacy than Charlotte wanted to handle.

Mr. and Ms. Popular. Every campus and every dormitory across this nation seems to have a couple people who *everyone* seems to know and adore from Day One. Don't let it throw you.

Lisa found it painful to see those around her with swarms of friends, sort of like going to a swanky restaurant on Valentine's Day by yourself. *"One guy seemed to have come to the university with half of his high school class. In the beginning, it seemed to me that everyone knew someone and I didn't."* Thankfully, after a couple initial days of feeling shell-shocked and isolated, Lisa began to meet more people and make friends. *"Everyone was so friendly!"*

• •

FRIEND IN A BOX: JUST ADD WATER!

While each friendship is unique, the getting-there is surprisingly predictable. Here's the quick version of what the young women interviewed found out about friendships as they started into their college careers.

Start with old-fashioned friendliness. Don't let yourself get trapped in insecurity or snobbishness. Be friendly to everyone. Even if you're having a miserable day, hide behind a quick smile and a bright hello. No need to frighten off a potential friend early in the game.

Remember, everyone is new. Everyone wants and needs great friends. That's a fantastic – and amazingly equal – jumping off point.

Your friendship landscape will likely shift. Just for the record, the majority of young women reported having a core of a few really close friends, then widening rings of casual let's-go-do-something friends and friendly acquaintances. Choose those closest to you wisely and well – they'll be your lifeline for years, if not decades, to come.

Your types of friends may change just as much as you do. You, your interests, and your activities are likely going to change in college. So may the type of friends that prove to be perfect for the College You. Don't dismiss folks just because they aren't like the crowd you hung out with in high school.

Follow your own path. What are your passions, or at least your areas of interest? Now if it's surfing and you are in Alaska, there's a problem. Otherwise, the solution is there before you. Attend meetings. Start a club. Go on outings. Have fun, and meet others who like the same things you do.

Give it time. Frequently it takes time to make good friends. It may be hard, but try to be patient and let things develop at their own pace.

Enjoy the little things. Sharing an apple on the way to class, giving someone a ride to the city, or taking a minute to review history notes just before the test are all excellent little steps towards breaking down walls. This is how people get to know each other, and how friendships are formed. Don't miss out on these opportunities by being oblivious or closed.

Guys make great friends. This could be old hat, or this could be a news flash for those that didn't have guys as friends in high school. There have been great reports from freshmen women who never considered a guy as a candidate for a friend. At the very least, it doubles your pool of potential friends!

Don't be intimidated by packs of seemingly great friends. One or more of them could be looking wistfully at you, thinking you look interesting. If you want to meet some of these pack animals, see if there is a low-key way to get to know them and find out if they really are good friend material. Or, be patient. In time you will be part of your own circle of friends, likely with other people looking wistfully at your pack!

Consider centering your efforts around mealtimes. There's a reason most socializing around the globe happens over food! Meals are an inherently social atmosphere, and people are usually in a good mood while eating. (If nothing else, you can bond while complaining about the dorm food.) If necessary, think of a plan (invite someone to join you at lunch, or put out pre-dinner snacks in your room and let things run their course) and go for it.

If new friends bring stress, get help. It happens. The transition to college is a great time and a stressful time. If the stress bubbles over for a friend (or for you) the best help is to get help. Your college will be ready for you. They've seen it before. Look around. Ask.

Tattoo this on your brain. Friendly is as friendly does. How very Forrest Gump, but true.

• •

Not Everything Greek is a Tragedy

Perhaps you were raised knowing you would pledge ol' Beta Beta. Perhaps you have no idea what that previous sentence means. Either way, welcome to the topic of sororities.

Tea soirees and toga parties. Beer bongs and secret candlelight ceremonies. Almost every college-faring female has some preconceived notion of what being a sorority member would be like. To many, the notion of being surrounded by a sisterhood that provides both a social life and philanthropic opportunities is thrilling. To many others, the inescapable conformity and restrictions that sororities represent sound like a walking nightmare. It's one of those truly individual decisions – one that you may have to contemplate before your first day of class, given the recruitment campaigns that start the moment you set foot on campus.

The actual rush process at most schools is pretty uniform. After all, it's a system that has been honed over the decades. In the beginning, rushees are invited to events at every single sorority house. As the sorority members get more familiar with the rushees, and vice versa, invitations come from fewer and fewer houses. Finally, the parties end and membership invitations (bids) are extended. It's possible to get one, more, or even none, depending on university policy. Those who decide to follow through become pledges, and get thrown into a period of non-stop Greek activity. While hazing is illegal in most states and prohibited on all campuses, it continues in various forms at certain houses. It could range from just a few truly silly activities to more emotionally disturbing options. Don't bother asking about these practices in advance, unfortunately, since the official response is always *"no hazing occurs."* You may not discover otherwise until you've taken an oath of secrecy and loyalty to the house. This warning isn't meant to be profoundly dire, by the way, just as a heads-up to the reality of what Greek life may contain.

What follows is a series of stories that represent every possible configuration regarding making the Greek decision in different college atmospheres. Some young women attended a school with a strong Greek system and decided to just join up. Some were at schools with massive Greek systems and decided to bypass the whole affair. And vice versa, and everything in between.

FIRST, HERE'S A USEFUL GLOSSARY

Sorority (sor.or´.i.ty) (n.): a society or club of females, especially in college.

Fraternity (fra.ter´.ni.ty) (n.): ditto. For guys.

Greek (grek) (adj.): Of or pertaining to a small Mediterranean country known as the birthplace of European civilization. Slang for a member in a sorority or fraternity. Civility levels vary widely.

Active (ak'tiv) (n): An existing member of a sorority or fraternity.

Pledge (plej) (n.): A new, probationary member of a sorority or fraternity.

Pledge (plej) (v): To join a sorority or fraternity.

Rush (rush) (n.): Events put on by sororities and fraternities to woo, entertain and observe prospective members.

Rush (rush) (v.): The process by which prospective Greeks make clear their interest in the Greek system as a whole and in their respected preferred houses; the process by which Actives observe and select their desired pledges.

GDI (n.): Goddamned Independent. Usually cheerful or tongue-in-cheek slang for someone who chooses not to join the Greek system. (All Greek houses are known by their letters.)

THE STORIES

HOLDEN - *Sorority membership on Holden's campus:20-30% of female students*

"I rushed to meet people. Since I was playing a sport, most of the people I knew were athletes or lived in my hall. I wanted a chance to meet people with different interests and who didn't necessarily live in my building."

Holden is happy with her sorority membership, but also finds it *"a bit outdated, and it's really hard not to laugh at some of the traditions sometimes. On the positive side, you meet a ton of great people, and it makes a big school a lot smaller. Mmmm…maybe too small. The parties and dress-up days are a lot of fun. It's important to remember not to center your entire life around it though."*

Sororities are serious business at Holden's school, which permits sorority residences to be located on campus. She finds the commitment fun, but seriously time consuming. With 20/20 hindsight, Holden would probably have made her school schedule a little lighter during the semester she pledged. Pledging involved unexpected calls in the middle of the night, weekend trips to other schools, and spending every waking hour at the actives' disposal. *"They will determine if and when you get to sleep."* Coping with rigorous sports practices and a full roster of games wasn't a problem, but it was joining a sorority that made her warn *"that you have to make some serious adjustments to your study habits. Expect your grades to slip.*

"If you have other serious commitments (sports, an a capella group, boyfriend, work, sleep), the balancing can be very difficult. If your group of friends doesn't join the same sorority, it's hard to keep in really close contact during pledging. Also your friends who decided not to rush feel left out. Sometimes [the sorority] makes you live in the sorority house your sophomore year."

Holden felt that for her, the disadvantages of joining a sorority were primarily time commitment problems. The three best things were new friends, constantly meeting new people, and the parties. Would she do it again? *"Absolutely."*

● ● ●

SARA - *Sorority membership on Sara's campus: 2% of female students*

Sororities and fraternities exist on Sara's campus, but represent a fairly insignificant part of social life and of the students at large. Sara's take: *"Something to laugh at."*

● ● ●

JOANNE - *Sorority membership on Joanne's campus: 25% of female students*

"Originally I rushed to make more girl friends and to find an outlet for community service [and] leadership roles on campus. [A sorority] seemed to offer many of those types of opportunities to its members that I would not get if I didn't rush."

Joanne's college permits national sorority organizations, but no actual sorority residences. Sorority members and non-Greeks live side by side in college residence halls. Joanne first learned about and researched the groups on campus, then rushed later. She is an active member of her chapter (president of her pledge class), and happy with her sorority life experience.

"[The sorority] really is everything I wanted it to be: a nice, friendly group of girls that are my friends, my resources, and my support system. But it isn't too overwhelming because we don't live together. Each girl is involved in the sorority as much as she wants to be based on her talents and schedule. That adds a really diverse angle to my group of friends. Not only have I gotten to meet a lot of people, but I have also been able to take on leadership roles in the Greek community and be involved in projects with the community that I otherwise would not have been able to participate in."

For Joanne, the primary advantages of her sorority life were learning how to work with peers in a semi-businesslike atmosphere; being exposed to many different types of people with whom she would be connected her entire life; and topical programs such as women's health and safety speakers, alumnae meetings to facilitate professional networking and philanthropy. As for disadvantages:

"Greeks have been getting a lot of negative press lately, and it is very unfortunate that the positive aspects aren't as publicized. We do such great things for the community and we are trying hard to fight that stereotype. Since our school is smaller than most, we have a distinct personality to our Greek system that most others cannot understand. It can be a very casual atmosphere that is based on mutual respect. Being Greek isn't branded on your forehead; it is very difficult to tell who is Greek just based on looks. And whoever said that Greeks are dumb needs to do their homework; our chapter has a 3.55 average GPA. That is higher than the all-female [university] average!"

Would she do it again?

"Yes, definitely! I encourage everybody to do it. If they decide it isn't for them, at least they gave it a shot."

●●●

SIMONE - *Sorority membership on Simone's campus: 2% of female students*

While Greek life exists on campus, there are far more fraternities than sororities. Simone felt that most of the sorority members at her school seemed like Hollywood typecasts. She decided to pass on the experience.

• • •

SAM - *Sorority membership on Sam's campus: 20-30% of female students*

In high school, Sam declared, ***"I was a conforming nonconformist."*** She would identify a social group who seemed to be marching to their own drummer, analyze what made them different, and then align herself to those norms and values. When campus life presented the opportunity to be classified, evaluated and accepted into a sorority, she thought about it carefully. Part of the equation for her was that Greek life absolutely dominated her campus – especially the social scene. Sam realized that her university wasn't very socially diverse, and the Greek system seemed even *more* homogeneous. ***"Non-Greek kids are never seen. There was guilt by association if you just hung out with Greek friends."*** However, Sam didn't buy into this guilt by association. ***"When you go to a school where others are different, you have a choice...be alike or be apart."***
  Sam chose to rush. To be "alike."
  She rushed in the spring of her freshman year. When she realized that her three best friends pledged three different sororities, ***"I chose a fourth...poorly."*** She hated the young women in her pledge class. Sam discovered the Greek system to be ***"...crap. Money buys friendship. Designer stuff predominated. Girls had no passion, no warmth, and were fakeand phony. Nothing inside them."***
  She completed pledging and then deactivated. For Sam, this was ***"when I felt free to be different."*** She started to feel increasingly comfortable with herself and her school. Her social life flourished outside of the ever-present Greek system.
  While Sam was content, she did wonder if she would have been happier at a university that was not so heavily Greek. She realized she had become ***"more of a liberal than I ever imagined."*** She regrets not investigating and applying to a college without a dominant Greek culture. It may have been a better fit.

• • •

KAREN - *Greek membership on Karen's campus: 2% of male students, 0% of females*

Like Charlotte, Karen selected her college precisely because there was a minimal Greek presence: no sororities and the fraternity system was small.As a student on campus, she grew to appreciate the social life that the weekly fraternity parties provided. ***"The [college] plays and concerts are great. But the [fraternity] parties! What fun!"*** Since the college is located in a small town, far from any signs of a city, this was a nice plus.

• • •

ANN - *Sorority membership on Ann's campus: 20-30% of female students*

Before starting college, Ann equated excess drinking and nonstop parties with sorority and fraternity life. And to some extent, she found this true. Her college – which has had trouble regulating its Greek system which is housed off campus and is autonomous from the school – acknowledged the drinking issue as a problem. And the college has redoubled efforts to create more events on campus so there are social alternatives to the drinkfests.

     With a year of college life under her belt, Ann saw sorority membership in a broader perspective. She noted that there is a large non-drinking, friendly, social constituency. Since life at her college is so Greek-oriented, Ann decided: *"…better in than out."* (This change in philosophy didn't apply to her attitude about drinking, however, which remained on her no-thank-you list.) Since money was an issue, Ann planned to become a R.A., and use the money she saved on room and board to fund her sorority membership fees.

• • •

VICTORIA - *Sorority membership on Victoria's campus: 20% of female students*

Discovering that her sorority experience was a source of discontent came as somewhat of a shock to Victoria, since she chose her college largely *for* its strong Greek system.

     Victoria didn't rush her freshman year, and made wonderful friends that grew to be a source of strength for her. *"Doing well in school and making new friends created happiness."* At the end of the year, she rushed and pledged. But sorority life wasn't what she had hoped. *"I find sorority rituals cultish, and I was surprised to find that a sorority is a business."* Violating any of the many rules resulted in monetary fines. Even harder to deal with was the fact that her fun and fantastic friends from freshman year lived together in the dorms way across campus, while Victoria found herself in a house filled with young women she has just met. *"This year not all my friends live together. Sometimes I feel isolated."* Regretting sorority membership, Victoria wished she hadn't gone through the process. *"I don't need the sorority."*

     There are practical reasons (most important, housing) to stick it out, and she intended to. But Victoria looked forward to studying abroad the following year, and to possibly make significant changes when she returned.

•••

LEILA - *Sorority membership on Leila'scampus: 20-30% of female students*

Greek life seemed like just another part of the experience to Leila when she evaluated her college options. When she finally landed at her school, she did contemplate joining a sorority. She got to know some members, but instead of being more excited at the thought of joining a house, she felt she simply had less and less in common with these women. Leila couldn't figure out how she'd fit in the Greek system. Ultimately, this discomfort was one of the reasons she transferred from her university.

•••

CHARLOTTE - *Sorority membership on Charlotte's campus:2% of female students*

When selecting her school, Charlotte sought out campuses where Greek life was either nonexistent or minimal. She just wasn't interested, and the tales she'd heard of drinking bothered her. Charlotte was happy with her college choice, and generally unaware of the small, albeit active Greek community.

•••

AMBER - *Sorority membership on Amber's campus: 20-30% of female students*

Sorority membership seemed like something Amber, a very active person on campus and generally a joiner, wanted to try. The enthusiastic reports coming from her sister, who preceded her at the college by two years and was a content sorority woman, gave Amber the extra impetus to give it a try. So she rushed, pledged and activated – and then deactivated just before Christmas break in her sophomore year.

Greek life was definitely *"the cool thing to do,"* but Amber also found what she called stereotyping: Sororities provided a place for everyone and everyone *in their place.* There was an abundance of rules and rituals. To Amber, the sorority spirit seemed just the opposite of the open, inquiring attitude that she thought college was supposed to foster. Looking back, Amber thought her sister's enthusiastic view of Greek life and devotion to it were distorted.

While Amber enjoyed sorority life, she was happier placing her energy in drama, an activity that also played a part in her bailing from her sorority house. The grueling rehearsal schedules forced her to postpone or forego sorority activities, sometimes distancing her from her house events for weeks.

Drama fulfilled her, so Amber committed more fully to it. Her sorority friends accepted her decision, and encouraged her to still attend all the sorority parties and keep in touch with her friends there. She did.

• • •

ALLISON - *Sorority membership on Allison's campus: 30% of female students*

Upbeat Allison loved the gorgeous sunny campus of her college and the beautiful people who inhabited it. The social life, epitomized by the sorority scene, seemed perfect. Allison decided to rush and become a part of it all. Coincidentally (or not) Allison broke up with her boyfriend just before rush began. *"Everything changed in my second semester. I joined a sorority. That was a major turning point. It opened up a whole social world to me."* Breaking up with her boyfriend *"...was hard. [As far as the sorority] to be totally honest ... with 40 girls there is a lot of estrogen It gets INTENSE. But it is still great. Great!"*

• • •

SYDNEY - *Sorority membership on Sydney's campus: 0%*

Sydney was very clear that she did not want a sorority or fraternity presence on her campus. Great. Done. But what she hadn't been prepared for was that there were other very powerful groups, which held sway over the campus social life, and which had slipped under Sydney's radar. *"What I don't like and neither do my friends is that in these[groups], people sort of purchase their friends."* The very tight, insular environment felt uncomfortable to Sydney. She was relieved that drinking and partying were pretty non-existent at her school, or at least conducted far outside her range of awareness. *"[My university] is different...less crazy because there aren't any fraternity parties. There is much less drinking, much more work. We have nerdy, dorky conversations and they're fun. [For fun] we play with Super-Soakers and Nerf guns."*

• •

WHAT TO DO?

News to you or trying to decide? Research. Visit the Web sites of the sororities on your campus. Try to get a sense of them, their activities, their characters and their values. Look for a decent fit. Remember that chapters of the same national sorority organization vary from campus to campus. Keep an eye out for individual member's personal Web sites at your college of choice. Surprisingly, several students report the least helpful in trying to get the big picture seems to be National Panhellenic, the central organization of the national sororities.

Many colleges are curiously silent on the subject of the Greek system. If you are still selecting a college, you might see what your top-choice schools have to say. Silence can be an answer in itself. If a university is not going to tackle the issues of Greek life (like hazing and excessive drinking) during the admission process, perhaps they will ignore problems after you are a student. Check it out.

Next take a step back. Consider the sorority scene as a whole. Comfortable?

Now think about the guys. How do you feel about the fraternities? You will be interacting with them, whether you decide to become involved in sorority life or not. Also, different sororities have traditional relationships with certain fraternities. If you join a group that always has events with hyper-brainy Alpha Alpha and you like the super athletic types in Beta Beta, sorority membership might prove to be counterproductive.

Look at your school. Check out the percentage of sorority membership: Anything more than 30% is going to be a Big Deal, 20% will be pretty dominant. Plan accordingly. Consider the impact of your decision to go Greek or bow out based in this context. Talk to more than one person about what the campus social life really is like and how the Greek scene fits into the university. (Are there tensions between the administration and the organizations? Is there a rampant drinking problem?) Round out the picture by talking to members and non-members, faculty and students.

The bonus of meeting people. Don't discount it. Even if sorority trappings and stereotypes are not your style, college is about people. So are sororities.

The parties. Really don't discount these!

The drinking. You know yourself and your preferences. Just be honest with yourself when thinking about how you'll deal with being in the thick of things. Also, run through the chapters on Sex, Drugs and Alcohol.

Does everyone get in somewhere? Maybe not, depending on your university's Greek policy. In these days of political correctness, some schools require that all rushees get admitted to at least one organization, even if it is not their favorite. Others let the elite groups go about their often brutal business of choosing and rejecting unfettered. Before plunging into the rush scene, it's worth asking what the policy is. Then, if relevant, ask yourself if you really want to risk the emotional trauma of rejection after bonding with other young women during the rush process.

Other groups. When researching a school, check out the other non-Greek groups on campus that may have the same social function as traditional sororities and/or fraternities. Your campus may have local societies, secret societies and dining clubs that are as strong or weak as any sorority scene. If you're already at college, put feelers out among friends and classmates and see what's up.

Not to be confusing. A residential college system doesn't fall into the same social category as the groups mentioned above, but they are a type of social organization that some universities use as a means to make a school more personable and personal. They might be described as "dorms with attitude." Residential colleges are frequently named for some illustrious benefactor or resident genius at the university. Affiliations may be determined by a busy registrar's office separating old classmates or randomly, literally by a lottery, or perhaps by declared major. Sometimes they are theme dorms (performing arts, international, smoke-free). Frequently, depending on the school, members of sororities and other social groups are scattered throughout the residential colleges.

It's your decision! The bottom line is that joining a sorority or any social group is your decision alone. Not your friends', nor your parents.' And while it may be hard to believe when you're in the thick of things, it really isn't that big of a deal. You can pledge and then deactivate. Decide not to rush one year, then change your mind and rush the following year. Throw yourself into a sorority without doubt, or throw yourself out of the path of any Greek affiliation without a doubt. All these options are all equally doable. It's all your choice.

Re-read the chapter you have just finished. Each young woman has a valuable story and experience. Whatever the situation at your college, think about sorority life and make the move that is right for you. It's your college career, which you know is about far more than books and tests.

• •

Mr. Right, Ms. Right-Now, and Mr. Whatever

Forget academics for the moment. Many key college experiences occur in the social arena. Think about it: No parents or bratty younger sibling waiting up at home. A huge array of date possibilities that don't include the boy who cheated off your spelling test in third grade. Frat parties, debate weekends, heck – even coed bathrooms. Let the fun begin.

And fun it can be. It's relatively easy to meet potential significant others (of whichever gender is your romantic preference) if you approach the college life with enthusiasm and your eyes open. Activities crop up at every turn, from the campus revival movie house to the local reggae fest. Of course, there is always everyone's favorite (and safe) first encounter, the "let's get coffee and study" semi-date. And don't overlook the enforced social opportunity that is the dorm laundry room or local Laundromat. There may even be a somewhat traditional dating scene on your campus, although the majority report is that official dates (regardless of who asked whom out) has pretty much vanished. Regardless, there will be suitors.

The *real* question is whether you want to date the hopefuls who pop up. (Welcome to the world of letting folks down easy, ladies.) Unfortunately, the reverse holds painfully true as well, and the crush of your life may not be interested. Then there are the "Mr. or Ms. Right-Nows," which are a blast. If you're lucky, there may be a "Mr. Right."

There's no predicting what a student's social experience that first year of college will be like. High school dating histories are, for better or for worse, not necessarily good indicators of what will come. For one thing, each school has its own social code and climate. (This is where colleges truly differ, far more than the more universal experiences reported regarding roommate issues and academics.) For another, *you* will be different than your high school self.

Read on to discover the most typical social scenarios reported by the young women.

NUMBER ONE SCENARIO: BOOM, THERE HE WAS

College twosomes take all forms – the one-night stand, the one-week fling, the one-month almost-love connection. However, it sounds as if there is a frenzy of matchmaking during Welcome Week at universities across the nation. The most common scenario reported by the young women was a quick plunge into a quasi-married state with their new loves-of-life.

But as much as many of these women loved being loved, most regretted their early entry into couplehood. It was too much, too soon. Given all the extenuating circumstances – adjusting to the rest of the college experience, getting to know themselves better, learning to be a better judge of character – most of these relationships had a short lifespan. Sometimes the person was great, but the timing was wrong. (From the safety of 20/20 hindsight, many of the women wished they had met their boyfriends later.) Sometimes the situations just got way too complicated, or even hurtful.

Take a look at these tales of how other young women navigated the always-tricky and sometimes rocky dating/relationship waters. Think about how you would handle these situations.

Holden met her boyfriend through a brilliant yenta stunt her grandmother pulled before Winter break. Her grandmother met another grandmother whose grandson just happened to attend Holden's college, 3,000 miles away. The two grandmothers giggled, said "what if" and gave Holden's address to Andrew with instructions to "say hello." Next thing Holden knew, the requisitely tall, dark and handsome Andrew was literally knocking at her door. Soon, it was love. However, Holden was a huge advocate of playing the field, meeting as many people as possible, juggling guys and going to every party possible. When she first fell for Andrew, they were together constantly at school, on vacations, and even met each other's families. While Holden loved Andrew, she wished she'd met him later on in life. A seriously committed relationship wasn't what she wanted right then. She missed her old social frenzy. It was *adios* Andrew six months later.

Ayla had a long-distance relationship her first year. She and Marc met at a summer job prior to college. He was an amazing man, knowledgeable and sensitive (he even liked to shop). The two kept the flames of love alive with weekend trips and outrageous phone bills. Sophomore year, Ayla transferred to Marc's school, partly in the name of love and partly because her visits showed that the school was a better fit for her than her original college choice. But six months later, the relationship was over. *"Every woman needs a room of her own,"* said Ayla, meaning every syllable.

Simone met Alexander casually in the fall, but didn't begin dating until February of their freshman year. Simone hadn't dated much in high school, and this was heaven. They had a wonderful relationship, but things were, well, *quiet*. When Simone was single her first semester, she hit the museums, restaurants and clubs at the nearby city nearly every weekend. Things were much more domestic second semester. Upon reflection, Simone supposed there was a certain social isolation that students feel when they allow themselves to commit to a boyfriend too early. She felt lucky to have experienced that first semester without a significant other, knowing she developed a better foundation for other friendships and got to better know the campus and nearby city. However, Alexander did help Simone get through what she called the *"sophomore slump."* The two remained together, but their social life became more active and inclusive with other friends.

Points to Ponder

Many early relationships don't last. Sorry, but it's the truth and it was probably meant to be, for a myriad of reasons. It may hurt, but it probably happens for a good reason. Chalk it up to one of those painful but inevitable learning experiences.

Committing your heart early in your college career can limit your options. Yes, having a significant other can be thrilling and feels wonderful. But spending so much time with one person limits the time to learn and grow with new friends and new experiences. This is a hard balance – many adults never get it right.

Boyfriends can open up new horizons. Part of getting to know someone well involves getting to know his passions, intellectual interests and friends. In Ayla's case, it even led

> **"**
> *Funny, most of my guy friends are virgins and are actually very unconfident in the sexual arena.*
> **"**
>
> ANN

her to a better college. Boyfriend perks abound.

Is he a crutch? Face it: With all the upheaval going on during the first semester of college, a boyfriend can be an emotional port in the storm. Maybe it was just simpler for both of you to transition to college with a steady heartthrob. Port in the storm? Is this what you have? Is this what you *want*?

DATING: IT AIN'T WHAT IT USED TO BE

Or sometimes, dating simply "ain't." That seemed to be a pretty popular response. The always-popular and ever-safe group activity abounds, but plain old-fashioned dating seems to have died off somewhere along the line.

Simone's careful analysis reflected the sentiment of just about every student interviewed. Dating as it was imagined, dreamed about and anticipated remains squarely in the fantasy world of "Dawson's Creek" and "Grease." *"From what I know about dating at [my college], it doesn't really happen. People generally fall into the following categories.*

> *a.) "Married, as I was for my first two years. This usually means that you don't go out socially without your significant other and generally go home early in order to pop a movie into the VCR and cuddle.*

> *b.) "Playing the field. This is not as fun as it sounds. Generally this means you 'hook up' [editor's note: read, have sex] with people who you either meet while going out with someone that you know casually or—sometimes accidentally— a good friend. This is followed by much laughter and discussion with your friends, but that is generally it. You may talk to that person on the phone once or twice and then see them the next weekend at another party where you may or may not end up going back to one of your rooms. Basically…no date or formal commitment is necessary for sexual contact. Occasionally, students can go in this pattern for a few weeks or months without ever talking to the person you are hooking up with whether or not you are actually 'seeing each other' or are monogamous. No one really wants to bring that up.*

> *c.) "In a constant state of talking about how there is no one to date on this campus and so there is no point in going out."*

Sam also reported that dating *"doesn't really happen"* on her campus. Parties absolutely do – there are plenty of fraternity parties. "Hook-ups" also abound, and Sam and her friends expressed a certain dissatisfaction with the casual and unloving quality of these relationships. *"I could easily say that dating means sleeping with the same person for an extended period of time."* Sam had never found *"the 'one' guy"* for her, nor had many of her friends and acquaintances. She maintained a philosophical outlook, believing that her college's social life wasn't a representation of the real world. In the end, Sam thought that ultimately, in school, *"people are later thankful for their independence."*

At **Holden's** school – one of the rare campuses where actual dating still exists – it's all about the social life. But even Holden recognized it as *"tricky. While it is a relatively large university, the social scene is very small. Be wary with whom you choose to get involved and to whom they are connected."* Holden once had three guys from one sports team calling her, unbeknownst to each other. When they found out (and this wasn't her idea) they all dropped Holden, who had moved on anyway. The guys remained friends and teammates with each other. Moral of the story: *"If you have a crush on [one] guy, make sure he is the one in that group that you really want because once you get involved with one of them it is probably bad taste and timing to pursue another."*

Joanne believes that singletons *"enjoy the freedom."* At her campus, while there were *"tons of couples that spend all their time together, studying, living, going out,"* she said that actual *"dates are very rare because there aren't that many places to go at night so you see the same people. Or people take their academics so seriously they are reluctant to make a 'significant other' a priority. Many students feel that they lose friends when they are seriously dating some-one, so those who chose not to date enjoy spending their times with close friends without the competition of their girlfriends or boyfriends."*

Having been in a long-term relationship since Day One at college, **Kate** could detachedly assess her school's relation-ship scene. Her observations were that *"my suitemates are involved in what we call 'random play' (just going to par-ties, hooking up once in a while, nothing serious) and I do think this gets frustrating. My close girlfriends just have not been able to find what they are looking for on levels including maturity, commitment and emotions."*

> **"**
> I could
> easily say
> that dating
> means sleeping
> with the
> same person
> for an
> extended
> period of time.
> **"**
>
> *SAM*

BUT WHAT ABOUT L-O-V-E?

Testing the waters and falling in love is one of the most exhilarating experiences in life, period. But as anyone who has survived to this age outside of a convent knows, it can also be a brutally painful time. Sometimes that right person just doesn't materialize when you need it, and friends telling you to be patient just isn't cutting it anymore. Sometimes exploring your sexuality can be socially and personally tough. Sometimes your room-mate's boyfriend is your soul mate, and there is nothing you can do to get a happy ending.

No matter what you want out of your college social life, odds are you'll find a group of like-minded individuals at college. Sex, abstinence, constant companionship or weekend fun, it's all there. Below is a collection of relationship tidbits from young women with different backgrounds and different expectations.

Who most matches you?

Outgoing and lighthearted, **Alexandra** lived for the moment. *"What makes me feel great is if the weather is sunny and I have a boyfriend."*

Ann had a boyfriend, enjoyed his company and the social life she had with him. *"When I met my boyfriend, my social activity really took off, [although] even before we were going out, I was having tons of fun."* They weren't having sex, however. Ann was far from alone with her attitude. She added, *"Funny, most of my guy friends are virgins and are actually very unconfident in the sexual arena."*

Kate, who went to an all-girls high school, declared *"I expected college to be a place to date like crazy and go to lots of parties. When I met Matthew I decided to table my dating and party plans because being with him was so worth it."* Kate and Matthew met during a pre-college orientation, thereby avoiding the pitfalls created by the inadequate social atmosphere Kate felt her college possesses.

Charlotte blew into college without a social agenda or a planned dating philosophy. She met Thomas, who attended another nearby university, around the end of her freshman year. Logistics were tough, but they both were initially willing to make the effort. The relationship lasted through the summer, then evaporated. It was nice while it lasted, but Charlotte discovered her college life was too full to accommodate the time it required for the commitment.

Sara and Brian were an on-again, off-again couple (of course this vastly oversimplifies the trauma involved) for the first two years of college. While she loved the security of a boyfriend, Sara also realized that *"I think I kinda got stuck with the person I was at the moment I met Brian."* During one of the bumpier, lumpier times, Sara came to this real-ization: *"I needed a life outside of my boyfriend; a sort of infrastructure of my own to support me and give me a sense of self outside of him so that I didn't NEED him so much."* Ultimately Sara and Brian split for good, and presumably Sara created her own infrastructure.

Sara added some sharp perception and sound advice: *"It's amazing how when you really don't need a relationship, they are not hard to find. I think guys can smell des-peration. All my friends that want a boyfriend (or a girlfriend) are constantly being dis-appointed. By the way, I think it's a myth that girls want a commitment and guys don't. My personal theory is that people tend to stay firmly in their own circle of friends and then look for love at bars, parties and clubs. This is doomed. I am sure if I hadn't hung out with different people over the summer when I separated from my boyfriend, my love life would be pretty dull as well. Meeting people is the only way to, well, meet people."*

So dating rarely exists, and hook-ups seem to be universally touted as unsatisfactory. Is there any good news here? Well, yes. As each young woman bumped along her own rela-tionship path, at the end, in her *"singledom,"* as Simone called it, she found strength and independence. And you will too. That is part of what college is all about.

NOW YOU SEE 'EM, NOW YOU DON'T

Guys come and go. So do relationships. (Serial monogamy a major component of modern campus life.) So does even the desire for a relationship. Often the normal state of affairs is a state of flux.

Kate observes that of the young women who are not in long-term relationships *"...the desire to be with someone comes and goes with our normal swings of emotions. ...they go through cycles of wanting relationships and not wanting them."*

Ayla had been in and out of relationships, and saw the time alone as necessary for personal growth and just attending to business, especially during challenging academic times. For her, *"... six months is about my limit, then I'm out again, scoping about."*

> 66
> ...dates
> are
> very rare...
> 99
> JOANNE

Points to Ponder

Am I ready to date, and all that it means on my own campus? Really sit down and ask yourself about this. You'll know. The trick comes in listening to the answer.

Do I want to date for the right reasons? Ask yourself. You'll know this too.

Sex is not a prerequisite to serious dating. Nor is serious dating a prerequisite to sex. You'll find both, which means you'll find like-minded people for whatever you're after.

UNFORSEEN COMPLICATIONS

One way that college creates a truly unique environment is that as you and everyone around you are in the middle of some pretty major personal epiphanies, transitions and transformations. Some of these folks (maybe you, maybe him) may have started in a fragile place to begin with. That can make for particularly dramatic relationship material.

Jane described her entire entry to school as *"fraught with despair."* Incredibly homesick and feeling isolated, Jane had just found a balance when she met Peter in the fall semester. They were simply friends at first, but the relationship evolved into something more the second semester. Jane had boyfriends before, but never one for whom she cared so much. She had never invested so much before. Love bloomed. But then things changed, as they are wont to do. Peter broke it off, which Jane classified as *"tragic."* She realized how much she had allowed herself to depend on him. Old feelings of inadequacy – which she had put on a back burner while with Peter –returned, and she felt trapped on an emotional roller coaster. *"My daily life was totally controlled by outside forces. … When the relationship began to crash, all those bad things magnified."* For Jane, the break-up was *"the straw that broke the camel's back. My head was spinning for nine months. I never got a grip."* Ultimately, Jane took a year off to reconnoiter. Mission accomplished. She went back to college and was doing fine.

> **" Don't look for someone and don't get involved unless it's really worth it. "**
>
> *SARA*

For **Sara,** it was her boyfriend Brian's emotional health that spiraled out of control. Brian, a nice guy from a Midwestern prep school, came into Sara's life during the first semester. While Sara had been content with her social life pre-Brian, she found college more enjoyable with him. Life was certainly not simpler, however. Under enormous academic pressure and worried about his scholarship, Brian grew severely depressed and dropped out of school spring semester. Returning home, he took a mental vacation, spending a lot of time hiking and outdoors. Sara hung in there with e-mails and good wishes. It was a tough time, but Brian worked things out and returned to school the following year. But when reflecting on relationships and their significance, Sara's advice echoed that of many other young women: *"Don't look for someone and don't get involved unless it is really worth it."*

Points to Ponder

Homesickness and feelings of isolation can stir up internal desperation. This can lead to alliances built on unhealthy foundations. Sometimes a boyfriend can become way too important. Seek balance.

When friends and loved ones have serious personal problems, you can be sucked into their whirlwind. Careful here. Recognize what's happening, while it's happening. Hang tight, and seek help for yourself if you feel you need it.

EXCUSE ME, BUT HOW *OLD* ARE YOU?

One of the most tragic discoveries most freshman women make is that the boys don't magically become men in the months between high school and college. Sorry, ladies, but the male maturation process takes time. (Not that this should be a news flash to anyone.) And while you may be past the Adam Sandler-like humor that filled high school, odds are it will take the guys a couple more years to move on.

Sam reflected on it this way: *"...as amazing as the girls at [my school] are, the guys are very immature and slightly restricted by their fraternity life, which makes them have huge egos. Even though they are actually insecure. I think that most girls here have either given up on finding a boyfriend here and are just enjoying the single life and the random hook-ups that come with it."*

Three of **Kate's** roommates echo these sentiments: *"[They] just have not been able to find what they are looking for on*

> **"**
> My suitemates are involved in what we call 'random play' and I do think this gets frustrating.
> **"**
> KATE

levels including maturity, commitment and emotions." Many of Kate's friends are guys, either friends of her boyfriend or just plain friends. She observes that most of these guys are not in relationships either. *"I think some of [the guys] are looking for some kind of meaningful relationship, but others are just not ready."*

Joanne lamented the rather homogeneous nature of the available dating pool at her particular university. *"For the most part, you better make preppy, smart, boy-next-door, cute, immature, boys be your type or you are out of luck."*

Points to Ponder

Guys can be immature. Nope, not your imagination.

The dating choices may be rather homogeneous. This certainly doesn't apply to every school, but it especially isn't surprising among the smaller colleges. A certain type – be it preppy or more hippie – is attracted to your school's particular character, just as you were.

• •

A ROMANTIC'S GUIDE TO DATING ...OR NOT

Even if you're rushing off to the romance waiting for you right around the corner, pause. Read this first!

If chemistry is ruling your heart, it probably won't matter what you read. Even this. But hey, we worked hard on this chapter!

On the other hand, let's be blunt. Doesn't 18 years old seem a teeny bit early to be pseudo-married? What's the rush? Isn't the point of college to grow? Doesn't that imply change? Think about how you may be limiting yourself by getting so deeply involved in your first week, first semester or first year.

Are you trying to recreate the familiar intimacy of home and high school? If you're falling into this trap, take a step back and think. Is a relationship really the best way? Or is love a quick fix substituting for a deeper and more meaningful look at your self? You can create your home, your comfort and your stability without using someone else as a crutch. And you'll be happier in the long run.

The first won't be the last chance. So you never dated in high school, and fear that the first guy might be the last. Highly unlikely. It's a big world out there, and you will be many people's dream partner. So if it's love, congratulations. But if it's panic or loneliness, you owe yourself more than that. Don't compromise.

You've had sex for the first time. And it's great. There is no judgment here, just a suggestion. Have a plan before you get intimate. Be prepared and smart. (Also, read the chapters on: Sex, Drugs and Alcohol.)

He's the only guy who doesn't demand sex. And it's great. But same as above: Have a plan before you get in too deep with this person. Your arrangement may keep life blessedly simple, or it may end up frustrating. Sorry, folks, there's never an easy answer. So be prepared and smart instead.

The downside of relationships. When significant others have personal problems (depression, death in their family, illness, academic trouble and more), you can easily be sucked-in, sometimes further than is wise. Of course, reaching out and helping those close to us is exactly what great relationships are about, but as in all things in life, maintaining a balance is the challenge. If you are backed into a corner with just one soul mate, it is easy to lose perspective. Are you taking on more than you get out of this relationship? Or is that too simple?

The bottom line. Do what *you* want to do, *when, how and with whom.* Your choices about drinking, using drugs, and having sex must be guided by your own moral compass, personality and good sense. But you already knew that.

●●●●●●●●●●●●●●●●●●●●●●●●●●●●●●●

SINGLE GENDER SELECTIONS: IF YOUR MR. RIGHT IS A MS.

For those already sure about or just starting to question their sexual orientation, college is ground zero for getting to know yourself. As you can imagine, the needle on the accept-o-meter tilts wildly depending on the particular college. The trick, of course, is to find an environment where you feel comfortable. With 3,000 colleges to choose from, a college that is open and friendly to homosexuals and bisexuals – while still offering the top-quality academics or the major collegiate sports scene – is out there and easily findable.

If you are already attending college and find yourself in the middle of the discovery process, you will likely have some difficult moments. Common sense says to go slowly until you get wired into local perspectives. Hopefully, there will be acceptance all the way around and you will be able to emerge in your own good time.

Although none of the young women contacted in the survey indicated same-sex interests, they did have some interesting observations about their various schools.

"Homosexuality is widely accepted here," Ayla wrote in response to the question, echoing the norm. *"I have a number of close friends as well as quite a few acquaintances who experience this lifestyle or a similar one (bisexual). They rarely come to me with concerns about acceptance."*

At **Simone's** college, *"…it is sort of so accepted that it [homosexuality] is really a non-issue. There is a significant population of 'out' members of the college community. Same-sex couples feel comfortable walking around together holding hands, and expressing affection in public…. In general I would say that the queer community (as they often refer to themselves) are a thriving and integral part of the school."*

Joanne, who attends a top-tier private school, indicated it just wasn't a topic for her or for friends. *"I do not know anyone who is gay, nor have I heard any stories."*

For **Kate,** at her ultra-large public university *"…[homosexuality] isn't a presence….I do know two homosexual people personally and they certainly do not live in fear or persecution from day to day, but neither of them are universally 'out of the closet.'"*

Scarlett believed that *"homosexuality is accepted in theory at my school although it hasn't been embraced by the whole community."* She went on to explain that there are comfortable places for gays and lesbians throughout the campus community. *"The Gay Alliance, in my subjective opinion, has decreased in visibility although it still holds it annual 'Gay Day.' A former roommate has recently discovered her bisexuality and has found people she associates with to be quite accepting. One of the sororities on campus tends to be looked on as the alternative group and attracts a significant number of homosexuals and bisexuals."*

Anne B. offered insight from an all-women's school. *"I do have an opinion that my [all-women's college] has a [homosexual community] significantly larger than the average coed school, but with regard to sexuality and most other differences, I find the environment to be very accepting. As a straight woman I have never felt that my interactions with the lesbian or bisexual students (a couple of friends and the rest acquaintances) has ever been awkward or strained because of this issue. By the way, being at a women's college has at no point caused me to consider 'switching sides' nor have I felt pressure by the queer community to be something I am not, just the way I have never expected them to pretend to be what they're not. Some people have strange misconceptions about this, and I am not quite sure where it comes from."*

Lastly, **Sam** rang in with a report clearly in the minority. At her college, *"the social scene does not condone [homosexuality] and if anything there is complete denial of it. I am sure there are gay and lesbian people who would like to come out, but sadly I don't think they will do so until they graduate. ...Outsiders, those outside the norm, are clearly not included. The boys that are gay, some of them I know, are still in the closet and continue to have intimate relationships with girls to hide their sexuality. This would be the last place on earth to come out."*

IS GENDER AN ISSUE?

If sexual orientation is on your particular agenda, think about where your college or prospective college fits on the scale above, then make your move accordingly and at your own pace.

••••••••••••••••••••••••••••••••••••

· ·

Hook-ups, Random Play and Taking a Pass

No matter what your starting point, or what you did or didn't do in high school, college is a brand new beginning. If you want to have sex, the option is there and readily available. If you want to take a break, that option is open too.

The previous chapter tackled the concept of relationships. This chapter addresses a topic guaranteed to make parents across the nation shudder slightly: recreational sex. Hey, it's out there. Universities consider incoming freshmen to be adults, and bestow upon them the corresponding degree of freedom. Residence halls tend to be co-ed, and the concept of no guys allowed in women's rooms after 10:00 p.m. flew out the window in the '60s. College social life offers up many attractive objects of physical affection. Depending on your philosophy, this could offer a bonanza of opportunities. But don't make the mistake of believing that everyone is "doing it." They're honestly not, as you'll see in this chapter. And unfortunately, don't underestimate how much you may find yourself emotionally hurt by a partner, no matter how much it all seemed like fun and games at first. The trick is to know yourself and know what you want. Everything else should fall into place from there.

THERE FOR THE TAKING

No parents will be frowning, and no curfews looming. Privacy abounds. Desirable guys or gals are everywhere – in the quad, living across the hall, doing laundry, sitting in the café, or studying next to you in the library. If you want a little action, opportunities abound. Just remember that you're *always* in the driver's seat when it comes to making decisions about *your* sex life.

As **Lauren** unequivocally summed up: *"There is much more sexual freedom in college."*

Condoms were seemingly available everywhere both on and off of **Simone's** campus. There are cubicles for them in the health center and at the post office. *"Some Resident Advisors put condoms [in makeshift containers] on the dorm doors."*

"I'm more of a risk taker socially," admitted **Joanne** about college. Joanne was very serious about her academics but she also allowed that increased sexual freedom (among other things) was part of what *"you can only find out about when you are a student."*

HOOK-UPS AND SPECIAL FRIENDS

Idioms abound for sex. There's the most common phrase of "hooking up," which can mean anything from a little action to the whole shebang. Then there's "random play," which is pretty much hooking up on a more, well, random basis. And then there are those "special friends," also known as "friendship with privileges." The emotional relationship is purely platonic, but the physical one is anything but.

Holden relayed that *"The best advice I received before I went to college was do not hook up with anyone in your hall. Although it can be extremely convenient, it would be a major source of awkwardness later on if or rather when it doesn't work out. …If you absolutely feel compelled to, I would recommend trying to restrain yourself at least until second semester when you have a better feel of the campus and of the scene."*

> **"**
> **…sex just makes life confusing, so stay away from actual intercourse.**
> **"**
> ANN

As she progressed through college and grew older, **Harriet** discovered that she was more open to having sexual relations without the benefit of a relationship. She had lots of guys playing the role of good buddies, and *"[there were] mostly casual hook-ups rather than relationships."*

Holden also came to believe, based on her observations, that while guys can be very good friends to women, *"guys all talk, a lot. Their loyalty is to each other."* Holden saw the entire issue of sex and relationships in a bigger context. *"Remember, these people are going to be your colleagues and bosses and subordinates later in life."*

NOT ALL FUN AND GAMES

Sex is a big deal, both emotionally and physically. While the sex-saturated media may trivialize what can be a very rich part of life, sex can and does usher in a host of complications to your life. It's truly O.K. – and truly normal – to be thrown for a loop.

Jeni found that the abundant opportunities of having sex for the first time could be confusing. As adults living away from home, things can happen so fast. Mental boundaries can be more easily crossed in the heat of the moment. *"Sex becomes scarier in college. [It's] easier for things to occur living in dorms."*

Ann and her boyfriend, who have a wonderful relationship, have decided to postpone sex indefinitely. Her view was that, *"sex just makes life confusing, so stay away from actual intercourse. Kissing is FUN."*

Coming from a relatively small prep school, **Lisa** discovered that at her ultra-large university it was hard to truly know the people she was interested in. It added a frightening aspect to sex and to meeting new people. She learned to be wary. *"You know, there's an issue about guys. They can be frightening. In high school you know everyone. In college, students come from many backgrounds. There can be problems, especially if alcohol is involved."*

Sam came out of an all-girls high school that taught the lesson that sex could empower women. Her college environment, however, provided quite a shock. The general feeling there was that *"sex was a bad thing. Girls felt subservient to guys; girls did feel like sluts after sex, and guys, who, for only self-appointed reasons, felt like gods, when they have really nothing going on inside."*

> **"**
> **[Abstinence?]**
> **Ummm,**
> **that wasn't**
> **exactly**
> **what**
> **I was going for.**
> **"**
>
> JANE

THREE LITTLE REMINDERS

Recreational sex. Yes, sex can be mutual sport, and it can be great fun. When asked about the idea of abstinence, **Jane** admitted candidly, *"Ummm, that wasn't exactly what I was going for."*

The nature of commitment. Often sexual relationships are born out of different motivations. One of you may be thinking casual; the other may be committing his/her heart. This is a common disconnect that can cause a world of hurt. **Sam** realized, ***"Too much of a good thing is a bad thing if your emotions are confused."*** Try to keep your radar up, and don't be afraid to ask your partner what he wants out of the physical relationship.

Safe sex. No matter which of the above two options you're going for, this is the constant. Even in this hyper-aware and educated day and age, it still may be surprisingly difficult to ensure that your sex is safe. **Joanne** realized she couldn't count on safe sex without the cooperation of guys. ***"Some do [agree to practicing safe sex]. Girls must be firm."***

● ●

TAKING A LOOK AT LOVE

Sure, most freshmen are familiar with and knowledgeable about the contents of Sex Education 101. You already know that getting pregnant is a very possible outcome of any sexual encounter, and that even protected sex can lead to contracting a potentially serious disease. Regardless, here's a tiny tutorial for things that perhaps you haven't stopped to consider yet.

The meaning of sex. What does having sex mean to you? Recreation? Pleasure? A search for love? For acceptance? A natural expression of romantic love? You may have already considered the above, especially if you're already sexually active, but college life presents a chance to reassess. If you need to talk to someone to get a clearer insight into where you truly, honestly stand about sex, don't be afraid to approach someone. (You'd do it if you were having a problem in your English Lit class, right?) There are always friends, older siblings, trusted mentors, or counselors at school who would be happy to listen to your thoughts and lend some perspicacity. Believe it or not, even your parents may have something interesting to say.

No glove, no love. If you choose to have sex, use protection. Period. You know intellectually that STDs (sexually transmitted diseases) and HIV can lurk in the cutest, smartest, most considerate lover. You know the statistics that one out of every three American college students are believed to be infected with some sort of STD. But in that delicious, hormone-filled moment, it can be so *easy* to forget or make an exception, or .... Snap out of it! Condoms are usually available for free in dorms. Go to student health services (where conversations are usually confidential) to talk about other means of protection. This is one area of life for which you can't make excuses to yourself.

Not everyone is doing it. While it may seem that everyone is doing it, that is simply not true. National data clearly reports that many young adults remain virgins for longer than you may suppose. In college you may actually feel less pressure regarding sexual experiences (or the lack thereof) than you did in high school. Say *adios* to the old cliques and *hola* to the much more widely embracing environment of college. Regardless of where the pressure comes from – a friend, yourself or a potential lover – make your decisions confidently and listen only to yourself. When it comes to sex, you might as well cherish the first time. There are no do-overs on this one.

●●●●●●●●●●●●●●●●●●●●●●●●●●●●●●●●●●●●
LIBBY'S STORY: WHEN THINGS GO REALLY WRONG

A very inebriated and sleepy **Libby** returned to her dorm after a party and crashed into bed. What felt like moments later through her fogged senses, she realized that an unknown, partially nude young man was sprawled on top of her. To her horror, Libby realized that he was fondling her. Her roommate was in the room, but sound asleep. Libby struggled to get out from under him, and in the process realized that this stranger had apparently passed out.

She finally got the guy off of her and fled the room. Libby immediately informed school officials, who summoned the local authorities. They found the young man, a high school student, chatting in the next bedroom. Police questioned him thoroughly.

Libby called home, and her father took the next plane to join her. Countless meetings ensued with school officials, police, therapists, attorneys and prosecutors. Despite Libby's account and the fact that he had left his underwear on Libby's bed, this young man was not prosecuted. Officials claimed the evidence was circumstantial.

Libby made it through her freshman year, but just barely. Her best girl and guy friends engulfed her in nurturing support and love. Over the summer, however, her fears returned and redoubled. Just before the fall semester began, she begged not to return.

Tragically, for Libby, school has become something to just endure. Libby mournfully warned, *"Lock your door. Don't trust everyone."*

Rape. If the worst happens, here are the facts.
Get help immediately. Call your Resident Assistant, student health services, campus security or 911. Ask your best friend tocall the police for you. Heck, call the darn Dean of Students if that is all you can think of. Just call someone immediately, and keep calling till you get someone who *will* help.

You'll probably have feelings of self-blame. Don't listen to that misguided inner voice. Other people may also try to blame you. Don't listen to them either.

Talk to a therapist who specializes in these issues. It doesn't mean that you're a weak person. Even if you think you're coping brilliantly – and you may be – nasty remnants of this trauma can surface years later if you don't deal with them now.

You'll be doing other students a favor if you report the whole incident. Keeping quiet may give your attacker a chance to harm someone else.

• •

"Just Say No"
– Who
Are They Kidding?

Animal House. *Road Trip*. We've all seen the movies. College can be a 24/7 party, filled with all the sex, booze and drugs a curious spirit could want. Universities have official policies against alcohol and drug use on campus (and we'll throw in for the record that it is illegal to drink under the age of 21 and to do drugs) ... but who are they kidding? No parents. No curfews. The abundantly available alcohol lowers inhibitions when it comes to experimenting with drugs and sex, also both are readily available. College is practically *synonymous* with experimentation – which by no means is necessarily all bad.

All things considered, humans figure out their limits and preferences through experimentation. For some, the experimentation may involve a single sip of beer to confirm that drinking is not for them. Others may explore the far side of the spectrum. Some experimentation is healthy, *required* even, for that much-talked-about passage to adulthood. However, as you well know, it's easy for too much experimentation to go wrong. The stakes are high because the problems are very real: addiction, rape, DUIs and wicked hangovers. It's important to keep perspective when it comes to any of these 'social consumptions,' and be open to the idea that help may need to be sought.

On that note, read on and discover what some of the young women's encounters with substances and hormones were like.

ALCOHOL: IT'S PARTY TIME

Across the board, alcohol seemed to be the most common substance – and springboard into other – "party substances." Although some students drink at high school parties for years before they get to college, the mere fact that it is so much easier to get your hands on a drink (or two or eight) changes the scene. That, and the lack of having to hide hang-overs from parents the morning after.

For **Alexandra**, alcohol was her substance of choice. She admitted to having had *"many encounters with binge drinking."* In addition to the obvious ramifications, she stumbled across another very common one: weight gain. Alcohol is one of the Freshman Fifteen's best friends. (See chapter on food.)

Like many college freshmen across the nation, **Ann** owned up to the fact that *"I drank for the first time this year. I realized it isn't poison, but you shouldn't drink to get wasted."*

Lauren found that *"unlike high school, where pot was the substance of choice, alcohol is preferred in college."*

After steering clear in high school, **Lola** embraced social drinking in college. Her favorites included the cheapest beer around *("yuk")*, generally available at frat parties, rum and Coke, and Jello shots (that would be Jello made with vodka rather than water) when they were available at certain parties.

> **"**
> *...there's a different mentality... someone who drinks to get drunk and those that just drink while hanging [out].*
> **"**
> LEILA

Sara recounted an evening in a club with friends. She had a glass of wine and then a few swallows of beer. *"I think my drink was spiked. My friends had to carry me out. I am so glad I was with people who were aware enough to take care of me. A lesson to all the girls out there, watch your drink and always make sure you are with trusted people who will watch your back."*

Leila (who claimed modest drinking habits but an out-of-control nicotine addiction) found *"there's a different mentality from someone who drinks to get drunk and those that just drink while they're hanging with friends."*

DRUGS: THE PERVASIVE ACCESSORY

Lisa never realized *"how easy and common drugs are to get and to use. And so many people smoke; it's easier than I thought to get hooked."* She is now in the more-difficult-than-anticipated process of quitting smoking.

Jane found that harder drugs cropped up everywhere. Pot. Acid. Ecstasy. Cocaine. K (a horse tranquilizer). Speed. Nitrous oxide. *"Mmmm, I guess I never saw heroin."* The second semester, her suitemates (but not her roommate) had more drugs than she'd ever seen before. Every morning, canisters of nitrous oxide were scattered on the bathroom floor. Jane experimented, then stopped when she realized it wasn't really for her.

Every month **Ayla** took a couple of hits of marijuana – which was always available – to mellow menstrual cramps. *"I've smoked pot, for medicinal reasons."* She got relief, but the downside was spacing out during class and midterms. Ayla finally went to an M.D., and is attacking the problem scientifically.

Like drinking, many of those who got in too deep with marijuana found it made sense to back off. The most frequently cited reason was academic performance. **Leslie** found *"marijuana is very prevalent recreationally, but even those who use, realize limits."*

It may sound simplistic, but **Ann** believed the use of drugs was easily controllable if you *"just say no."* For her, this held true. As for cigarettes, they were *"disgusting."* She laments, *"How can people who are so smart do things that are so stupid?"*

THE SIREN CALL OF CURIOSITY

The fact that **Harriet** was well prepared academically turned out to have an unexpected implication – she had plenty of time to experiment, and experiment she did. In hindsight, she admitted to believing at the time that she was prepared to handle college life and all its implications, but *"mostly I didn't always make the best choices. I was interested in trying everything."* Binge drinking, sexual freedom, and recreational drugs became pastimes. She was used to having wine with family dinners at home, but *"at college it became more about getting drunk."* Once vehemently opposed to cigarettes, she soon hung out with smokers and smoked occasionally herself. However, after getting a little perspective

"

*And
so many
people smoke;
it's easier
than I thought
to get hooked.*

"

LISA

over her first semester break, Harriet hoped for a slightly calmer lifestyle during the rest of her college time.

• •

PERSPECTIVES ON PARTYING

The Bottom Line. Alcohol and drugs are going to be easily available and possibly high profile at college. Substance use is your choice and yours alone. The best advice is simply to be aware of what you're doing. Draw your own line in the sand wherever you're comfortable, then try to be alert to whenever you cross that line. Have fun as responsibly as possible (remember, surviving the college years is always a nice idea), and if you think you need help, get it! That said, here are a few precautions.

Inhibitions. Alcohol and drugs lower inhibitions, paving the way to unwanted and/or unprotected sex, and all of the attendant problems that can bring. Feelings of invincibility also mount, leading to such suicidally (or homicidally) reckless behavior such as climbing behind the wheel while not sober. More young adults die in alcohol-related automobile accidents than in any other manner.

On a less dire note, lowered inhibitions can lead to other things you don't necessarily want to do, like smoking (a clinically proven fact), overeating thanks to the munchies, or starting a fight. Just something to think about.

Binge drinking. That would be drinking pretty much drinking until you drop. And then some. Students can and do die from alcohol poisoning. More frequently, they just throw up a lot, feel crappy the next day, or hook up with some guy they didn't really like. Honestly, who needs to deal with all that?

Addiction is possible. When a habit becomes a necessity, get help. The sooner, the better. Be extra-sensitive to this problem if other members of your family have had addiction problems.

Drugs and alcohol won't help your grades. There's really no way to argue this one.

Drugs and alcohol won't help your sports performance. Can't argue this one either.

Mixing friends and alcohol. There is a distinction between friends who hang out and share a few drinks on a lazy Saturday night and friends who only get hammered whenever they're together. Think about whether your drinking buddies are actually friends. You may want to reconsider your social agenda if you're not sure of the answer.

Smoking. It's a documented health hazard, not to mention some seriously gnarly tooth discoloration.

P.S. A lot of this is illegal. While the college administrators may turn their collective heads, local police may be more rigid in their outlook. Jail time and a ticket home is always possible.

P.P.S. Most sexual assaults experienced by college students occur in situations involving drinking or drug use – by the victim, the assailant or both.

What's a girl to do?

- Decline.

- Alternate glasses of water with every alcoholic drink.

- Sip slowly. Roughly one drink per hour keeps most women nicely buzzed without getting wasted.

- Become allergic. It's easy. Just say, "Oh, I'm allergic."

- Be aware of your limits.

- Make sure to eat before drinking or using drugs. Food acts as a buffer, slowing down (but not stopping) the inebriation process.

• •

Methods Out of Madness

College is, quite simply, the Mt. Everest of time management. Sure, you worked hard in high school and have a decent handle on how to juggle your commitments and fulfill your obligations. But no matter what your situation was like, high school life was still pretty well structured. There were full class days and carpools, extracurricular meetings and hot meals on the table. In contrast the utterly unfettered experience of college days can be intoxicating, intimidating or both. And it will be different than what you're used to.

The following chapter looks at some of the most common hurdles the young women found they had to clear on their way to establishing a satisfying and satisfyingly ordered college existence, and their favorite tricks that made it possible.

NO MATTER WHAT, THINGS *WILL* CHANGE

Karen had the monumental but fundamental realization that hits every college student early on: *"Gee, there's no structure."* There was free time galore. There was time between classes to nap, time to party on weeknights, and time to play academic catch-up on days with no classes.

As a high school gymnast who balanced daily practices with a heavy school load, **Scarlett** brought exceptional time management skills and boundless motivation to college. Yet once there, Scarlett also found it *"easier to waste time because the schedule was not as* *regimented, and there were more erratic hours."* This extended to eating habits as well. *"I would snack all the time. (Yes, I gained weight.)"*

Sara found that for her, studying in spurts instead of the daily grind a la high school generated a certain amount of anxiety and stress in her life. Her solution was to muddle through regardless. She fell back on her high school training; kept schedules in her day-book, planned times to study, made timelines for researching papers, for writing papers for studying for tests, and made exercise a priority. It was still a tough act to pull off. But hooray. It worked. Good grades. Happy freshman.

Even though procrastination and high school went hand in hand, **Lauren** not only dealt well with the pressure it created, she liked it. But in college, it was a whole new ball game and *"procrastination became even more of a problem."*

FINDING THE BEAT OF YOUR OWN DRUMMER

The answer to handling the gaping days for many of the young women interviewed was to assertively set up their lives to their own beat. Each one has her own tricks, quirks and needs. Just figure out what you need to do and what you *want* to do, and the rest should fall into place.

Her first semester, **Simone** found her college schedule chuck-full of holes during the day. She filled the time with volunteering several times a week at a house for adolescents dealing with gender and sexuality issues.

At first, the freedom of setting her own sleep schedule outweighed the pain of sleep deprivation, but the scales inevitably tipped. Simone decided to grow more regimented in this area. *"My mother wasn't there to make me go to sleep at 3:30-4:00 a.m., so I had to set limits for myself in doing work."*

Gee, there's no structure.

KAREN

For **Lisa,** the hardest part of school was balancing the academic workload and the social panorama that lie tantalizingly just outside her dorm room window. She finally realized that there would always be a party, but the library and computer labs had finite hours. That gave her a basic schedule that still left time for everything. The best part was *"there was always someone to study with."*

Instant Messenger so captivated **Lola** that she had to escape her dorm room, along with the other wonderful and usually welcome distractions of online chat rooms, the telephone, radio, TV and friends dropping by. Studying in the library became her most effective alternative.

Although the freedom to skip a class or lecture here or there sounded seductive, **Arielle** also had heard that this was the Number One way to land in a real academic mess. Preemptively, she decided to go to every single class, which proved to be a good strategy for her. *"I went to every class and every discussion this semester so that when I went back to talk to the current seniors at my high school, I could say that such a feat is possible."*

For **Karen**, attending religious services proved to be an important – if surprising – part of the life she was creating for herself. The weekly nondenominational vespers services she favored not only allowed her to explore her growing spirituality, they also offered a great way to meet new friends and visit old ones. Her still-evolving spirituality came as a surprise to Karen, who came from a family that believed in a supreme being but not organized religions. *"I feel like at college I almost crave spirituality. It's weird."*

THE INS AND OUTS OF SLEEP DEPRIVATION

A good night's sleep has to be one of the greatest experiences on this planet. Yet when thrown into the whirlwind of academic pressures and social flurries, a decent amount of sleep seems to be the first thing that flies out the freshman door – especially in the early months of the semester. But without sleep, you're going to be exhausted, feel cranky, look kind of haggard and be prone to illness. The body feels free to punish those who abuse it. Consider sleep a crucial part of time management, and clear your schedule for it.

Instead of academics, her social life proved to lie at the root of **Leslie's** time-crunch problem. *"Having access to friends 24 hours a day made it tempting not to sleep. After half of the semester I learned to sleep enough. Before that I kept myself miserably tired."*

Arielle became ill early in the first semester, which she took to be a sign of where things were headed. She promptly put herself on a schedule, getting eight hours of sleep a night. She's been fine ever since.

Scarlett took another approach towards getting all her work

> **“**
> **My mother
> wasn't there...
> I had to
> set limits
> for myself ...**
> **”**
>
> SIMONE

done: *"I learned how to pull all-nighters."* To counterbalance this, she tried to get her "normal" amount of sleep on a cumulative basis, adding up naps throughout the day. Scarlett believed this trick worked for her and is a decent balance.

Naps earned rave reviews from **Holden** and many other women as the key to getting by on minimal sleep. But as the first semester progressed, they reported, the idea of a regular night of sleep grew increasingly attractive. For what it's worth, every single woman interviewed reported that whatever their initial behavior was, they reverted back to the soothing normalcy of cozy pajamas and a comfortable bed for as many hours of sleep as they could get.

BUILDING STRUCTURE

There are the countless familiar components – sports, hobbies, discussion groups and friends – that go into building an active routine in life away from home. But one not-so-obvious area that the freshman women said was an important addition to building a happy college life also emerged: part-time work, be it a paid or volunteer position.

Scarlett took a campus job her freshman year. It wasn't too serious – she proctored a game room several afternoons a week, where she was as much a participant as a supervisor. The pocket money certainly eased the starving-student life, although her parents hadn't requested that she work while in school. Scarlett felt that the job helped make her transition to college life smooth and enjoyable, giving her some of the structure she enjoyed in high school.

In search of activities, **Charlotte** (the art major) tried crewing. It seemed like a good idea considering she was a water polo enthusiast in high school. Alas, the year-round training program for collegiate crewing proved too demanding. She then decided to use her free time for work. She soon found a tedious job in the slide library her freshman year, which at least afforded her an opportunity to meet professors and helped her prepare for art classes. Charlotte moved on to work at the student gallery, which proved to be the perfect fit. She helped plan and organize programs, and is surrounded by student, faculty and community art lovers.

> **" I learned how to pull all-nighters. "**
>
> *SCARLETT*

Feeling the need to create structure in her life, **Karen** began tutoring students from low-income schools, which she had done and enjoyed in high school. She also set aside time for modern dance classes and a dance extracurricular group. Karen also loved parties, and learned to schedule time for them too. Fraternity parties predictably rumbled out onto The Row every weekend, a welcome addition to campus life in this remote college town.

• •

MAKING IT WORK

Accept the fact that there is very little structure in college and deal with it. Classes are your only firmly scheduled commitment week in and week out. That leaves a ton of flextime, which can be both a reward and a nemesis. Be prepared for this fact.

Create a schedule. You have the freedom (and the time) to do whatever you want. So do something – be it continuing high school pastimes or finding new ones, committing to a volunteer or paid job, or even becoming a study or an exercise fiend. Just remember to show up to class regularly too!

Know that you can't go to every party. So many parties, so little time. It's sad but true. Studying has to be your primary commitment in school, unless you want to land a job that involves asking if customers want fries with that. But don't worry: For every party you miss there will be many more you attend. It just comes down to a tad of self-discipline.

Figure out what your distractions are. Is your personal demon e-mail? Or is it all-night gabfests or getting sucked into fashion magazines? Whatever your distractions are, try to be analytical here. If you need to go to your special place to study, then do it. If you're efficient in what you have to do, it will actually give you more free time in the end.

Get sleep. Sure you'll go a bit wild when freshly landed in a dorm, but you're going to need sleep at some point. Your brain and your immune system will thank you. You might as well figure out how to best fit it in, and try to stick to your preferred routine.

• •

HOLDEN: CLUES AND VIEWS

"Don't burn bridges. The guy who doesn't show [on a date] or the girl who breaks the academic curve could end up being your boss or your boyfriend."

"Don't hook up with anyone in your hall."

"Keep an open mind. Get involved."

"Join the college gym. I pay just $50 a year. Great way to meet guys too."

"Power naps: Take them when you can."

"The great thing [about dorm life] is no matter what time of day [it is], someone is awake."

[As far as graduating in four years] "I'm staying as long as possible."

• •

VICTORIA: CLUES AND VIEWS

"Take classes for learning sake."

"Sleep!"

"Eat healthy."

"Get your studying done."

• •

● ●

AMBER SUMS IT UP: A SNAPSHOT

On a lazy, sunny day Amber leaned back and pondered in what ways she had changed since high school. Her off-the-cuff replies, below, are noteworthy for being pretty typical of the freshman experience. Consider it a snapshot of a college experience.

On education: *"[I've been] very mellow about [education], learning because I want to, not because I have to."*

On sex: *"The same. OK before marriage, but [I'm] still cautious."*

On drugs: *"More exposed to it, but still not into the scene."*

On alcohol: *"Never drank in high school, now I do moderately. I definitely could have gone overboard, but I was not sheltered from it in high school so I did not feel the necessity to rebel."*

On cigarettes: *"Never touched one."*

On sleep: *"Naps! For the most part. I feel more healthy today than in high school."*

On parents: *"Now I'm closer with Mom, can talk to her more."*

On religion: *"Gradually, since 10th grade, [I have grown] more spiritual and [simultaneously] further from any sect or institutional religion."*

On career goals: *"What you major in does not matter in the long run. The important thing is learning who I am and being happy with myself, what I study and my friends."*

On time management: *"I am still a procrastinator, but I manage."*

On the big picture: *"Find a school you can be most comfortable at socially. The academics will follow. If you are happy with who you are and your friends, then you will want to work more. Classes are what you put into them, so don't choose a college based on the name... every college has something to offer if you are willing to look."*

● ●

If You Like Airplane Food, You're Going to Love College!

Sorry to break this to you, but mystery meat and greasy pasta dishes are only a couple of the brutal realities that college food will introduce into your life. Complaints drove this topic, with downright negativity running a not-too-distant second. (*"Too many potatoes! I've become a very nutritionally unbalanced vegetarian because I'm too picky for what they offer." - Leslie, a vegetarian*)

But let's be honest – who really selected their college based on the menu? Also, while most college students complain about the food, no one actually leaves the school because of it.

Cafeteria bashing is an acclaimed, albeit unofficial, sport. Food is the college commodity students love to hate. People bond over it. Another possibly unexpected bonus is how downright-gourmet home cooking will seem during vacations. So cheer up.

While the food may range from the dull to the horrific, no one has been known to starve. On the contrary, this is where the famed Freshman Fifteen phenomenon comes in. And it does, relentlessly, no matter what your metabolism was like in high school. This happens largely because dorm food is generally not very healthy. Nor is the pizza, to which scores of students flock for refuge during late-night study sessions. Nor is that triple-mocha addiction you picked up somewhere along your sleep-deprived way. Be aware, and try as always for balance. (*"I should have avoided the all-you-can-eat buffets." - Holden*)

Everyone knows how they *should* eat and exercise, and both were probably fairly easy to achieve at home. In college, it becomes more a question of discipline and creative thinking. (*"You have to be very creative. Discover the salad bar."* - Sara)

Dorm residents usually are required to sign up for one of the university's various food plans. Every college has a different food plan scheme, but general options usually include the "every-meal-every-day" category, the "once-a-day" category, the "weekday-only" option, and some middle-ground choices. The plan acts as a pre-paid food coupon for a residence hall's cafeteria, and possibly for various campus eateries as well. What you do is an entirely personal choice.

Also, keep in mind that some people really do find the food acceptable. Boredom with the options may be the culprit, more so than taste. You're one of the lucky ones if family meals weren't that great to begin with. (*"I like the choices at school better than at home. It's all in what you are used to! The food is repetitive, but it's good. I love the desserts and dance off the calories."* - Sophie, a vegetarian)

• •

TRIAGE FOR CAFETERIA-RELATED TRAUMA

Carefully consider the food plan options. You may be able to switch categories once the semester is in full swing, but check it out in advance and read the fine print. Many colleges make it easier to move up a notch to more meals per week, but not to cut down. (Remember, they're running a business here.) While you may find the food repulsive, having a pre-paid meal plan means you'll never starve – even if you're broke. Also, find out if you can use your meal plan card for credit at on-campus eateries, which can seriously expand your menu options.

D-I-Y. If the food is simply inedible, see if you can Do-It-Yourself. Find out if your college will allow a small refrigerator, a hot plate and/or a toaster oven in your room. Some universities have arrangements with companies that rent mini-fridges to dorm residents, and have safety guidelines that spell out which brands of appliances are allowed. The next step is to check with your roommate. She may already own a crucial appliance. If you can get in touch with her ahead of time to plan, do so. If you can't, be prepared for possible redundancy. And read the roommate chapter for other helpful strategies.

Stock the fridge with snacks, or even think about cooking yourself. (No, that sound is not your parents laughing in disbelief!) Invaluable secret weapons include **rice cookers**, which got rave reviews from several students interviewed, and **cookbooks**. There are appropriately titled cookbooks dedicated exclusively to college students. There will most likely be a collegiate- minded cookbook section in your campus bookstore.

Shopping. In case you've never done the grocery shopping on your own before, lesson number one: Junk food and junk snacks are not only generally not nutritious, they're comparatively expensive as well.

Budget for food flings. Allocate some funds for eating out, late-night sustenance and groceries. You'll be glad you have the latitude to skip the dining hall on occasion, which can make the whole dining experience more palatable.

Befriend the pizza guy. Seriously. Which does bring us to …

The dreaded Freshman Fifteen. It may not be 15 pounds exactly, but think about the late-night eating, the cheesy, starchy comfort foods that everyone craves sometime, the lack of sleep and exercise, and for some, the calories packed into alcohol. Those extra calories have to go somewhere, and it's usually not in a place you want it.

Locate the salad bar. Admit it, you know what you *should* be eating. While occasional indulgences with the curly fries are fine, try to balance it out with the universal salad bar.

Consider protein and green leafy things your friends. Just watch out for the high-calorie salad dressings and toppings.

Find the gym. Colleges usually have them, and they are usually great. Exercise classes frequently are free or cost a minimal fee. So hit the Stairmaster as an alternative stress reducer to that Kit Kat bar. Another plus is that the gym is filled with fascinating, dateable men and women. Can that Kit Kat bar claim the same thing?

•••••••••••••••••••••••••••••••••••

Dazzled, Dazed and Confused ...Welcome!

Welcome to the brave new world of college academics. Prepare to be surrounded by engaging, inquisitive classmates and inspiring professors who stimulate your own intellectual creativity. Prepare to be dazzled by a wealth of courses in fields you've never even heard of before in your life. And then, prepare for the possibility of being surrounded by intimidatingly brilliant classmates and snobby professors who take the my-way-or-the-highway approach to teaching.

Ah, yes. Welcome to college academics.

Some students will sail on in, confident that high school has prepared them well. Others may be nervous about how high the bar will be raised. Some may eagerly look forward to having stimulating discussions with fellow bright students, all the while the professor smiles encouragingly at such insight. Some may be fearful of those killer curves and cut-throat study practices.

So which of the above type of experience is the norm? You guessed it ...both. College academics will be easier than expected at times, and will kick your tail at other points. The material will be more rewarding than you ever knew school-related work could be, and will also put you to sleep without fail during that pesky post-lunch lecture. Then there are those headaches sparked by trying to figure out prerequisites and requirements, how to get into that over-subscribed class, or how you're supposed to stumble upon the perfect major.

Take a deep breath. Don't get overwhelmed. Now is the time to think through what you want to get out of your college academic experience. Anticipate some of the potential pitfalls, which will ease your way simply by forestalling you from walking into a new situation completely blind. See what some women have encountered in the college classroom, and how they've tackled what college academics has thrown their way.

AN INTELLECTUAL BOUNTY

The most prevalent comments and the most significant reports coming from the young women interviewed concerned the dazzling intellectual banquet college served up. Classes were exciting, and course choices were awesome in their breadth. Campuses inside the classroom and out felt downright alive with intellectual energy. Here are some of the tales that emerged.

Alexandra personified the boundless intellectual freedom most of the young women found at college. In fact in some ways, college exceeded her expectations. *"In high school I didn't feel I really knew how to think independently. High school never encouraged it. In college, professors are dedicated. Kids want to learn, they're smart and intellectual."* Education, she said, *"it's what you make of it! It's a job, just be interested in the material."*

Upbeat **Ayla** was exuberant when describing the joy she took in her work. *"I feel so very lucky. My classes are awesome. I sit in the front row of every class and feel so very on top of it. Freud. What a smart guy. My prof is supposedly one of the top three experts in the country. Funny guy too, I like his humor. ...I think I'm top of the class. I'm very proud of myself."*

Simone was utterly absorbed by her classes. *"They are challenging, frustrating and satisfying."* She found the course work, which tends to be conducted on a more abstract level, tougher than in high school. The work and the process were intense, and she can almost physically feel her analytical thinking grow. The key question wasn't "what is the answer," but rather "what do you think?" Frequently the answer was simply, "what is the question?" She observed: *"The students are very smooth intellectually."* This translated at times into excitement in the classroom, and at other times became a game of intellectual power-fencing. Reporting with a grin, she described a common event: *"two students vigorously debating a book, and neither of them have read it."*

It was the range and depth that **Sara** found to be exciting. She found classes in topics, whole fields even, that she never knew existed in high school: Hydrology, an entire major built on the study of water; Cognitive Science, a cutting-edge field fusing linguistics, higher mathematics, and the psychology of learning; Medieval Studies; Molecular Biology. The list was two pages long. In tiny type. Each class was taught by experts in their individual fields. Most held doctorates. Graduate teaching assistants were far enough ahead to have significant expertise. It was exhilarating for Sara.

For **Lola,** the unique mentoring system at her college was responsible for sparking her intellectual curiosity. First-year students signed up for a course that interested them, but was not necessarily in their major. In fact, most students had no idea about a major at this point. The teacher of the chosen course became that student's first-year mentor.

Selecting the class in a rather point-and-click manner, Lola drew, quite unintentionally, as her teacher and mentor, a petite Jewish lady from Texas. Dr. Spelling (Jane to Lola) chaired two departments, was multi-lingual, and a scholar. Lola admitted that she had yet to fully comprehend this woman's diversity, but adored her and considered her relationship with this woman one of the best parts of the transition into higher education.

A key part of college is the professors you'll encounter. While Lola's college forced the issue, you'd be missing part of the overall experience if you didn't get to know one or more of the faculty members as a friend or mentor. Professors tend to be fascinating people, who are often in a position to offer very sound guidance. They've almost seen it all. You might think of them as your own personal board of directors. These friendships can last long after your the diploma is granted.

Four years simply not enough to milk the college experience for everything it's worth? **Amber** figured ways to cram in more. She planned a double major – and then some. Her first major was known colloquially as SAL – a combination of science, art and literature – and the second was Art History. She also intended to spend the Spring semester of her junior year in Italy as part of her Art History degree. Amber's forecast: *"It's going to take me five years to complete my degree."* This was just fine with Amber, who was too in love with learning and having too much fun to squeeze everything into four years just to finish on a someone else's preconceived schedule. Lots of people take five years to complete a double major. A fifth year may be something to consider to achieve your objectives, assuming you have a willing partner to bankroll the endeavor.

> **"**
> **In high school
> I didn't feel
> I really knew
> how
> to think
> independently.**
> **"**
> *ALEXANDRA*

For **Scarlett,** academic life proved to be everything she dreamed it would be, but what really took her breath away were the intellectual opportunities outside the classroom. She attended small discussion groups, some required and some optional add-ons to her schedule, and found them stimulating. She also happily took advantage of the veritable parade of renowned authors, thinkers, dancers, Pulitzer Prize winners and politicians who spoke or performed on her campus.

Scarlett was one of many to make this discovery. Indulge in everything your college has to offer your intellect. Life after college certainly won't be like this.

Points to Ponder

Don't be standoffish or ultra-cool. Jump in. Take what your college offers both in and out of the classroom.

Participate in class. This will be good for you. Enjoy the uncertainty. Welcome new ideas. Take advantage of every morsel that is there. This is a unique life experience.

Participate out of class. Another world of wonder, just as important as the official in-class learning process. One off-the-record idea: If there is someone you'd like to hear or meet and it doesn't look like they will be coming your way, do it yourself! Hook up with a campus club or events bureau to sponsor your invitation. You'd be amazed at what the cachet of a college invitation can accomplish.

Take advantage of the faculty. Burrow in and find out what they have to offer individually and collectively. You will find an amazing community of minds.

SURROUNDED BY EINSTEINS

Brace yourself. After attending high school and ranking respectably in your graduating class, it's a shock to learn you are finally surrounded by your equals – at the very least – or perhaps students more gifted than you. Even if high school was high-powered, the spectrum is shifting. There is always the bottom half of a high school class. In college your segment of the class is probably right there with you. The other guys are elsewhere. Probability: you'll feel the competition of equals, maybe for the first time.

Bad news here: You're not going to get out of this potentially anxiety-provoking situation, no matter what. There is more probably going to be more brainpower floating around on a college campus than you've had floating around you in the past.

Consider this. Suppose *you* were in the bottom half of your high school class. Part of that bottom half crowd went to their least demanding collegiate option. And if you went to that least demanding option, you can bet there will be plenty of students who are there for other reasons; a great music department, stand-out biology professors, or not being able to afford Option A. Remember, many of the kids who didn't like studying just packed it in after high school graduation. Result: repeat, there is more brainpower floating around on a college campus than you've had floating around you in the past. Just be prepared. Don't let it top out your anxiety level.

Indeed it was a surprise to **Karen**, pretty much a smarty herself, to find at her university so many students even smarter than she. She reminds herself that at her highly focused prep school, academic life had been a *"never ending cycle of pain and fatigue."* When the intellectual going got tough, she would just look around, pedal harder and ultimately prevail. So when she thought about it, college was not so different, even though it wasn't easy. Yes, classes were more sophisticated. More importantly, the intellectual neighborhood was different. The students wanted to be there and were all quite purposeful. She hit upon the same solution: Pedal harder. Academic demands grew more manageable for her for several reasons. Karen became so used to coping with the demands of school that it was engraved in her psyche. Also, like most students, she had more free time to study and play in college.

In the same vein, your own performance may surprise you given the new context. **Leslie**, who was well prepared, enjoyed school and had all the SAT numbers on her side, worked hard. But some of the required classes were lackluster, even if her electives were inspiring. She still plowed along, worked hard, and *"did the best she could."* Despite these efforts, Leslie was disappointed with her semester grades, some of which were plain poor. She looked around at her classmates. Was it the curve? She resolved to check out the curve, and re-evaluate if she was taking the right classes for her. She also pursued sensible study strategies, such as talking to professors to find out what went wrong, play a little less, study a little more, and get more sleep. Leslie was determined to get her GPA up to her personal standards, curve be darned.

Points to Ponder

A universe of smarty pants! No matter what your rank in class in high school, this ratcheting up of the intellectual net is something you are going to have to deal with in college. Time to strategize and create a plan that will work for you.

> **"**
> **The students are very smooth intellectually.**
> **"**
> SIMONE

Good news! Out in the real world, including the work world, the air won't be so rare. And you will have learned a lot about the world and relationships and all the good things that college has to offer. You'll shine again, probably even more brightly.

THE OCCASIONAL SNOOZE-CRUISE

Surprise, surprise. College classes can be utterly, entirely, and downright boring. That's right, boring. After years of expecting that classes would be challenging, even difficult, some women were thrilled and some forlorn with that reality.

Yes, the core classes or general education requirements have their problems. Sometimes other classes will be boring as well. For better or for worse, **Jane** didn't find any university classes challenging. In spite of missing classes, she did the work easily and achieved high marks. This isn't always the case.

Even **Holden**, who was intellectually stimulated beyond her wildest dreams, admitted: *"Yes! Schoolwork is tedious sometimes."* Holden's solution: Hunker down, study harder, pretend the class is interesting. Maybe pretending will make it so. Like kissing a frog and hoping for a prince. If the situation called for it, Holden pulled an all-nighter if that's what it took to get through the class and the boredom.

Stephanie hit on another problem. Sometimes a professor's extensive experience translates into too much experience. Knowledge doesn't always make for interesting lectures. Hold the details of the details, please! Consider this: profs are just folks laboring away at a job. What intrigued them at 20 may be stultifying at 40, the downside of tenure. They themselves may be bored, burned out with giving the same lectures year after year, or maybe more interested in their research and publishing issues. Your last test or term paper can literally seem sophomoric to him or her.

Keep hold of this reality check: Most professors have a low tolerance for slackers, real or imagined. Could that be you? Think about it. And sometimes, professors will be abrupt and just plain rude. Rude? Yup. They are mere mortals. And yes, you will survive.

Points to Ponder

Keep working. Keep your head down and your chin up, or something like that. Don't quit. Workload has a nasty habit of snowballing if avoided, and the situation will only get worse.

To keep boredom at bay, think: what can y-o-u do? In addition to the thoughts above, consider turning into the campus Sherlock Holmes. Do research to find out who are the good, or even great teachers. Winnow out what makes a good, or even great class. Talk to friends, folks in the major, the guy or young woman next to you in lecture hall or your dorm. You can maximize the razzle-dazzle in your education.

STRESS, YOUR SOMETIMES COMPANION ...

Life can be swimming along just fine, then suddenly your stomach hurts by day and your headaches by night. Little wisps of anxiety drift through your brain. Could this be stress induced by academics? *Moi?* Well, maybe. Even the staunchest, strongest students recounted, at some point, hitting the academic wall. When it happens it hurts. And stress, in whatever form you favor, can bubble up.

Lauren never anticipated how much work she would be called on to do. Clearly she was a good student. Still, there was this huge workload, which was an enormous surprise. Lauren pushed through the workload in the same old-fashioned way that solved her other problems: She strategized. She worked smarter and harder. She still felt stress, but figured it was a part of college life. In lieu of bubble baths (a high school favorite) she took long, hot showers.

In her experience, **Ayla** felt as if she had been dowsed by a bucket of cold water. A high achiever in high school, Ayla was expecting college to be more of the same, if maybe kicked up a notch. Oops. Kicked over the hill was more like it. Ayla had never worked so hard and gotten so little. She dropped some classes, and galloped to catch up in others. In some cases she never did catch up. *"[Neither my] parents, nor I understood the academic pressures and expectations. They conformed with the [university] standards, which I felt were unrealistic."* Ayla decided it was time to bail. She later became a dean's list member at her new school. Well, that was one way to handle stress.

Ann had a more cavalier outlook. *"Of course, there is academic stress. But is goes away. Stress comes in waves. Once I had three tests in three days and a paper due."* Yes, there were *"lots of opportunity to experience lots of emotions, goodness and badness. This is a good thing. I don't regret*

> **"**
> *I don't regret
> the stress
> or
> the frustration
> with both
> academics
> and friends.
> I figure
> I'll learn
> from it all.*
> **"**
>
> ANN

the stress or the frustration with both academics and friends. I figure I'll learn from it all." Ann's roommate suffered a great deal of homesickness that first year, *"and she is a very tense person. Helping her actually reduced my stress."* Ann was also a member of the strategize-and-buckle-down school of stress reduction. It certainly worked for her.

Points to Ponder

Yup, it's hard. That's why your degree is going to be valuable. You could even make a case for believing the harder the better. But right now you probably need encouragement, not philosophy. Take a look at the Study Strategies section coming up in this chapter.

Yup, it's hard but you can do it. The admission committee had faith in you. Either your grades or your board scores or your recommendations worked for you and your university and they made a decision, based on plenty of experience, that you could do it. You're going to be fine. Keep working. Take a look at the Study Strategies section in this chapter.

....OR NOT

Let's take a step back and look at the whole picture. Say you take 15 or 16 units (four or five classes depending on whether it's a semester or quarter system), which is a sizable but average load. Three or four hours per week per class plus roughly two hours of study for every hour in class, plus extra discussion groups.

Forget it, you do the math. This is more important. Yes, college takes up a lot of time, but hardly the kind of time you'll be putting in for the post-college job market. And hardly a dent in the kind of time you spend skiing for a week. Not to mention, this is less structured time than high school. Yes, sometimes it's mind-bending to look at all your commitments, but you'll learn to take it in stride. So loosen up. Do your work, then enjoy life. The stress will evaporate.

Say, are you taking yourself too seriously? **Ann** admits *"Somehow I imagined constant intellectual conversations late at night. This happens occasionally, but at dinner I can't say we're breaking new intellectual ground talking about the college dean's new haircut."*

Leslie spent her previous academic career in fast-track private schools, and found college pressures to be almost liberating. *"College is much more liberal and relaxed about aca-*

demics...in college there was no punishment for poor grades." In elementary school, she remembered teachers yelling at students for not turning in homework. This started a lifelong reaction in Leslie. *"I don't like to be stressed. Academics can't give meaning to life. I don't think high school kept that in perspective. Life doesn't revolve around classes and work. Yes, you should work hard, and worry about the future, but don't forget to have FUN."* So while Leslie worked hard and did the best she could, she felt freer in college and had enthusiasm for her classes. And she happily pursued life experiences outside of the classroom.

VOCABULARY LESSON: C-O-R-E

If you haven't heard about core courses, also known as general education requirements, you soon will.

Core courses are how schools lead you to water and pretty much force you to drink. Take one class from this list, and three from that list, and so on and so on. These are the central hurdles you have to clear for your degree. While they can be a total drag and stress-inducing, most young women interviewed had an overwhelmingly positive attitude towards core classes.

Here's how it works. There will be a list, and a complicated list and a long list, of academic requirements. The requirements can include, for example, two classes each in Natural Sciences and Humanities, one class in Multicultural Awareness, and one in Social Sciences. Or you might be required to take History of Western Thought or an overview humanities section among other selections. It's a menu from a wild and crazy Chinese restaurant. Yours to indulge.

Sara picked from her college's requirements. She enjoyed the across-the-board sampling of knowledge. And slowly, the required core courses were being checked off. Then she looked forward to the more specialized classes in her major.

There is a dark side here, which **Stephanie** saw clearly. Most of her core classes were quite large and way too impersonal, even in her ultra-nurturing private, liberal arts environment. They were more given to rote learning rather than innovation and exploration. She found them repetitive, rather like warmed over, uber-high school classes instead of college.

"
I can't say we're breaking new intellectual ground talking about the dean's new haircut.
"

ANN

Listening to **Leslie** pointed the way to conventional wisdom and probably some good ideas. Get the core or general education requirements out of the way early. Several reasons. First, it is possible that one of these core classes will introduce you to a field of study or ideas that will chart the direction for your college career or your life. Also, you won't be taking Speech 101A with a room full of freshmen on your way out the door in your senior year.

Here's another common issue with core classes: Having to take a class from a discipline that is already "no thanks." As in, "Yikes I thought high school was the last of science/Spanish/calculus" or fill in the blank. Maybe an Advanced Placement class back in high school would have done the trick. Too late for that now. Strategies for coping with your current reality are listed at the end of this chapter.

Points to Ponder

Reality check. You are going to have to fulfill the core course or general ed requirements both for your college and your major. Submit. Enjoy as much as possible. You will absolutely learn something, and might even find a fervent new interest.

Expect some bumps here. Take the long view. And take a look at the course catalogue to search for alternative ways of fulfilling the same core requirements. Maybe instead of Introductory Physical Science which bored you in both eighth and ninth grades, you will find Introductory Geology more interesting. Perhaps there will be protracted educational field trips, like Costa Rica during Spring break or Western Canada during ski season. Be open. Be imaginative.

And once you pick a major, check those requirements. Check with the curriculum advisors in your chosen department.

THEY *DO* SAY TIME FLIES

Guess what? There are usually no academic check-ups in college for quite a while into the quarter or semester. Remember high school's constant routine of homework, quizzes and exams? While you know intellectually that things are different in college, it's still easy to get blindsided. And that first midterm is usually a doozy, in part since you were just so darn busy getting into the full, fun swing of college life. Don't start justifying; it happens to almost everyone.

So plan on six to eight weeks – depending on whether you are in a quarter or semester system – before your first test. And plan on it being a biggie. Maybe there will be a few papers, problem sets or labs building up to the midterm, but not necessarily. The bottom line is that you need to make every grade count.

Here is where the stress really kicks in. Everyone, parents included, ask "So, how are you doing?" You probably don't know, and don't even have a vague grasp of where you stand yet. Consider leveling, at least with your parents. Sample reply: "You know, I don't know how I am doing in school and I won't know for another six weeks." You might add "I'm worried," if you are.

Sara was exasperated. ***"What did these professors want?"*** In the first meeting, the professor handed out his syllabus. There was a reading list that looked monumental and completely unreasonable. There were test dates, oh so far away. No details. No idea of what was expected. And no conversation about expectations. The lectures started in like a lawnmower and just didn't stop. Direct questions were met with vague answers. Sara wanted to hide. In fact, the temptation to skip class to alleviate this stress was powerful. Skipping class led to guilt. Guilt led back to class and to studying with a vengeance. This led to more stress and so on, all of which was alleviated when the grades came out. After riding the upward spiral of stress, Sara did just fine.

Kate too, needed the grounding of examinations and evaluations. The road ahead was clear *"after the first set of midterms."*

Points to Ponder

Keep working and stay current with your work. You'll be fine, but understand it will take six to eight weeks to prove it to yourself. Don't let up in the interim.

Be candid with yourself. Did you take on too much? Drop a course. Drop it as soon as you know it's a goner and you can spend more time on classes that will get you somewhere. Or drop it right up to the deadline. But drop it. That's what you do in college when the work is too much. Don't get a poor or failing grade. It will take years or never to put your grade point back together after an F.

Any slack, pick it up later in your college career. College

> **" Yes, you should work hard and worry about the future, but don't forget to have fun. "**
>
> *LESLIE*

will get easier as you go along. The first quarter or semester is the most difficult simply because it is so unknown. The work becomes easier to handle with every passing class and every day. All this is obvious, but easy to forget or not fully realize on your way in.

HAVE YOU HEARD, ANGOLA IS NICE IN THE FALL?

Whether you're interested in beating your own path in the Congo or following the path along Paris' Left Bank, you'll want to consider your school's study abroad program as early as the first month of your first year. Advanced planning is necessary to take advantage of this unique off-campus opportunity, be it for a semester, a year or a summer. Start researching prerequisites (like language proficiency) and transfer credit rules as soon as possible, especially if you want to pull everything off in four years. Alternatively, many students – like **Amber** – simply make room for a year abroad by planning to attend college for five years. If you're even casually interested in studying in a foreign country or another campus, it's worth checking out early. The saddest words in college are "what if." Many students plan, go, and absolutely love the experience.

However, don't buy into the pressure if you're not interested. College life is a rich enough experience in and of itself. **Lola** felt this way after seeing so many opportunities on her campus. She felt no clear compulsion or goal that inspired her to take a junior year abroad. Sure, she could attend a great foreign university, learn a language and assimilate into a new culture, but Lola felt so lucky to be at her university that she didn't want to reduce her time there by flying the coop prematurely.

Points to Ponder

Consider. Do you want to go abroad as part of your college experience? Just because everyone else is doing it doesn't make it right for you. Does it sound right? For you?

Decide. If going abroad is in the cards for you, then make your plans. There will be plenty of people to help you. If you even *think* you might want to take advantage of the opportunity, make plans as if you were going. It is simpler to back out than to start in late.

Double check. Make sure classes you take abroad will transfer and apply toward your particular degree requirements. This is especially true if you are counting on graduating in four years. Recommendation: Don't trust the first "yes." Get it in writing. Sounds like a pain, but so is coming home for your senior year to discover nothing has transferred. Apparently this happens. A lot.

While you're at it. Plan ahead for a place to live when you return! A dorm room, an apartment or a friend's couch. You're going to have to sleep somewhere.

Plan ahead. Start planning as soon as your tush hits the seat. That would be now.

● ●

FACTS FOR THE EDUCATIONAL FAST TRACK

Here it is; the lickety-split version. Tips for academic survival if you're in a hurry.

Partake of the intellectual banquet that is college. There it is. Go for it. Enjoy the classes. Dig in. Enjoy the extracurricular lectures and symposiums.

Your roadmap through college is the catalogue of classes. Get it. Read it. Use it. The catalogue will help unravel the academic requirements you need to get your diploma. And more than that, it is an overview of the wide array of opportunities on campus.

Plan ahead. Good advice for life, and essential in college. Get the catalogue. Chances are solutions to your academic planning puzzle will be there.

More planning questions? The counseling center is there to help you. What do you want? See what you can arrange.

Expect to be expected to think. Spoon feeding is not going to be offered on your college or university campus. Use your head and common sense. These helped you get into this school in the first place. It won't be easy in the beginning. You're smart. You'll get the hang of it.

Expect to be expected to study as you go along. Know that in college there won't be little quizzes and grading opportunities on a weekly or more frequent basis.

Be realistic about your classes. Some, to be blunt, will be boring. Don't stress about the required courses that don't fascinate you. Focus on the positive: Some or one of these requirements might just spark an interest lying hidden within you.

Consider getting basic graduation credits out of the way. You'll have to take them anyway. Why not now?

Maybe you won't be on the top of the heap, like in high school. Not to worry. You did just fine in high school. You applied to and were accepted at a dandy college or university, to be part of a population of like-bright minds. It's just this kind of intellectual stimulation and challenge, that engenders great learning. Lots of people have confidence that you can do the work.

Try not to stress. Pressure – internal, parental, peer, or other. Do your best not to stress. College is a path to learning and experience and should be valued just for that.

Get strategies in place. Read the Study Strategies sub section of this chapter. It will just take a minute. It will help. Honest.

So much to do, so little time. This can be a good thing. Four years of college could seem long, even forever, or a moment in time, but they are your four (or more) years. To repeat what Alexandra advised, *"It's what you make of it."*

PARTING THOUGHT

Make your plan. Every day is truly the first day of the rest of your life.

● ●

STUDY STRATEGIES: SEVEN TIPS

OK. You've read the women's tales and gained some insight into what college academics will really be like. But now what? The following section is a bit different: It hunkers down into the nitty-gritty, giving you concrete ideas about how best to tackle the mountains and the molehills of academia.

This collection of winning practical ideas were inspired by **Anne B.** and several other students interviewed. No promise that this is the only or absolute path to academic success – there are experts and other books for that. These are student-recommended strategies that will very likely make your school life more manageable.

Of course, every college has different rules. Make sure to double-check any strategy to ensure what will work – or is even feasible – on your particular campus.

Strategy number one: Figure out how to study for each particular class.

You may think you have this process down from high school. You have your routine, and it got you this far, right? Well, no surprise here, but college is different. There is no one formula to success, and old study methods may *hurt* rather than help. College classes – like the best high school ones – move away from sheer memorization and promote innovative thinking.

Anne B. noticed that *"some very smart kids are struggling because they do not have the study skills."* Other women reported students hunched over books, reading every single word for exhausting hours on end, and retyping notes to memorize vast quantities of material. Unless this is for one of those notoriously memorization-driven classes (like Intro to Art History), these students aren't likely to ace their exams.

Get to meet and know the Teaching Assistant (T.A.) for any class that you're not sure quite how to approach. Ask what exams are like, and what the professor truly cares about. For example, the T.A. may tell you: Forget about the summaries and the dates, just memorize the top three to five reasons for each battle. Or vice versa. Or this prof never actually asks for proofs on the tests, despite threatening to do so in class. The T.A. probably knows more about getting through the class than the professor him or herself does – especially if the T.A. is grading your work, which is often the case for larger courses. Of course, if there is no T.A., march up to professor and get the job done that way. They'll be happy to answer any reasonable questions. (Just don't "grade-grub." That usually annoys them profoundly!)

Strategy number two: Figure out which classes could be problem classes.

Then develop a plan to deal with it.

Joanne was set on being a doctor. Since her existing science ability was OK but not great, Joanne came to realize that the universally dreaded Organic Chemistry could become a make-it or break-it class for her. She admitted being *"frustrated by the feeling of being 'weeded out.'"*

    Taking all that into consideration, Joanne took O-Chem the summer after her freshman year at a local state college, where this class didn't have the hyper-competitive aura that it maintained at her own university. Prudently, Joanne figured out a way to clear this requirement without feeling weed-out pressure, and probably obtained a higher grade since it was her only class that summer.

If you do consider attending a state or community junior college to fulfill requirements, make absolutely certain that your university will accept the credits. Once again, get it in writing.

Another thought: consider taking a killer class for no credit at all during the summer in a more low-key environment. Repeat it at your college in the fall. You'll be a whiz.

Other strategies consist of scouting around departments and fellow students to discover which professors have reputations for running classes with a more welcoming environment or even a less stringent grade curve. Try to take the potentially problematic class with them.

Strategy number three: Investigate the pass/fail options at your school.

If you are like **Leslie,** you'll be ecstatic with the possibilities of pass/fail, something never a consideration in high school.

With pass/fail you can take classes and well, hardly have to worry about a grade. Are there restrictions? Of course. It's up to you to figure them out and make it all work for you. Study the course catalogue!

Another boon is the audit possibility. You take a class just to learn. No grade, maybe no transcript notation. You pay your fee and take the class.

Informal option: Drop by and speak to the professor. Ask if it would be a problem if you sort of inhaled the class from the back row, unofficially. No fee, no nothing. Odds are the prof will say yes. You will never read about this in the course catalogue.

If it is allowed, do any of the above and take the course the following year for credit. You'll be an expert, probably get a good grade and do wonders for your GPA.

Strategy number four: Meet the course catalogue, your new best friend.

Perhaps you perused the catalogue as you selected your school. Chances are you didn't. It will be thick as a large-type bible, probably with a colorful, playful, scenic cover. Treat it as your bible to college. Study all the small type, from page one onward. Figure out what your general education options are, what you want to explore, or even where you want to depart from the norm and take a course off campus. Sit back and go shopping. Course catalogues are written with unerring precision, and describe the courses and your options in excruciating detail. You may find it simpler to have a human guide for your journey. Head to the counseling or advising department and strike up an acquaintance.

Strategy number five: Really get to know your professor(s).

There are plenty of reasons to get to know your professors. Clearly, if you are having trouble in the academics of a class, this is right up there in Strategy Number One. Another reason to get to know them is they are probably interesting and certainly well educated.

They also have a lot of clout, formal and informal, on a campus. Can't get into a class? Go see the prof. Tell your tale of woe. He or she may make room for you and be flattered that you are interested enough to make the effort.

Professors can frequently make prerequisites disappear if they think you are, for some reason, qualified to take their class or would be an asset.

And of course, getting to know your professor is good on general principles. Suppose, for example, you come down with pneumonia during finals. If he or she knows you've been a good scout all along, you're more likely to get the benefit of the doubt and whatever sort of accommodating plan you'll need to complete the course.

Last but not least, do you really need to be reminded that professors in your major will frequently have connections in your chosen field? Do you understand that sometimes this is how you will get a j-o-b? Or get into graduate school? Certainly the goal of college is to impart critical thinking, outright learning and a complete education. But you'll probably be marching off to work after all these years of study. Make no mistake: You'll probably find someone in school or in class to help you on your journey.

Strategy number six: Consider making college a five-year stint.

Lots of folks go five years unintentionally, so why not plan on it? This assumes, of course, you have the financial firepower to stay that extra year.

Consider this scenario. (Here is where college administrators and registrars leave for the smelling salts. There must be a whole science about who and how many, take what classes and when. There goes the bar graph or the circle chart, right out the ol' bell tower!)

So, the scenario. Take a full load of courses, even more if you can make it happen. Then drop the most difficult class or classes or those that are dragging you down. That's right. Drop 'em. Careful though, as you go along. Keep enough classes to maintain your status as a full-time student. You want to keep the financial benefits (loans, scholarship, your parents' taxes) attached to full-time status. And keep a close eye on the deadlines to drop a class. Be careful not to find ugly surprises on your transcript because you let deadlines pass. There is a long recovery time from a wayward F.

Another caution. Some classes are offered only in alternate years and are prerequisites to yet other classes that are going to be required for your major. Ka Blam!. You could find yourself sucked in for six years if you don't plan carefully for the long-term. By the way, your university may not allow you to stay that long. Fancy that!

What does all this get you? Well, yes, you'll need additional on-campus time to complete your degree. But the bonuses are fewer classes per year, which hopefully means less stress. Certainly more time for fun, or for studying, or for both. Probably a higher GPA. Consider the trade-off and your personal goals. Decide accordingly.

Strategy number seven: Figure out a great combination just for you.

Now that you know about the general education requirements and strategies one through six, figure out how to make it work for you. For learning. For growing. And for just muddling through, when that makes sense.

• •

There's
No Place Like Home
... Right?

Scientific fact: The shortest span of time in college is the adrenaline-filled, life-altering stretch between the start of a new school year and Thanksgiving vacation. You've tumbled through the rabbit hole, made friends, possibly dealt with the first round of midterms, and are loving your freedom when – *hello* – it's time to head back home.

Back home, to life as usual. Back home, to the parents who are eagerly waiting to embrace their little girl again. This should be a snap ... shouldn't it?

Across the board, the young women interviewed found that returning to the nest was surprisingly difficult. They saw themselves as generally more open, sophisticated and mature. They could accept differing points of view, debate world issues, and had proven adept (thank you very much) at managing their lives and determining such personal details as eating patterns and bed times. In short, they felt like they were adults and should be treated as such.

And yet, you can bet that parents and siblings won't be in sync with this transformation. It's been a mere couple of months for them, while your life has been turned upside down. They have the same life, the same friends and the same personal philosophies as before. Your kid sister still has to be driven to ballet class, and someone still has to take out the trash, right?

So do yourself a favor and be prepared for the Thanksgiving experience, whatever it may bring. It probably won't be the event you imagined.

Isabel stumbled upon this surprising – and surprisingly common – source of stress. *"Thanksgiving was hard...it was difficult going home. Hard to be a kid again. Then it was hard to leave and go back to school."*

For **Lisa,** her experience at home proved to be so hard her freshman year that she decided to not go back for Thanksgiving her sophomore year. She happily went to a friend's house instead, and felt that she had finally broken the bond to childhood.

Ann similarly found it difficult to return home for visits. She felt smothered, having grown used to her independence at college but still forced to follow the house rules. *"I love them, but I get frustrated. I need more independence."* The chance to stretch her wings at school meant that her position in the family household shifted. Seemingly no longer the *"center of [her parents'] universe,"* Ann realized that she was *"more willing to fight with them. They need to realize that I am an adult. I love them, but when I go home, I don't need my mom telling me what to eat for lunch and how to cook it."* Moreover, her conversations with her parents grew more guarded. She told them that she had a boyfriend, but not *"that I have slept with (but not had sex with) my boyfriend."* Ann realized that she longed for a closer, more trusting relationship with her parents and thought she would tell them *"everything, as long as they didn't make judgments."* In other words, her parents also needed to make the transition to accepting Ann as an adult in her own right.

Joanne also chafed at the difference between her life at college and home life. She thrived on the freedom her school life afforded her. In fact, she was surprised, *"how easily I [got] used to complete freedom."* Returning home for vacations and summer breaks meant that curfews, rules, and running unwelcome errands for the family became realities again. The summer after her freshman year was filled with suffocating parental pressure and concentrated study for a chemistry class she had decided to take at a local university. Joanne realized that this would be the last summer she would ever spend at home. Angry and disappointed, she believed that *"if your child is not ready to be on their own at age eighteen, they may never be."*

> **" They need to realize that I am an adult. I love them, but ... "**
>
> ANN

There are positive experiences, of course.

Sam may have balked at the old curfew and rules she dealt with when returning home for the occasional holiday, but college had taught her that her parents *"had done a good job raising me."* She still wished that *"they didn't worry so much,"* and believed that she has *"become more mature than they are."* But the visits were rewarding in their own right.

Lisa was downright joyous when describing the best perk of all when visiting home. *"There I could shower with my shoes off."*

● ●

STRATEGIES FOR RE-ENTRY

Face it: If those who have gone before report back that returning home can be problematic, odds are you may face the same issue. Perhaps simple awareness that difficulties may emerge is half the battle. It still helps to have some strategies at the ready.

Try communicating. All those great communication skills you learned when coping with roommates and new friends at college? Remember? Try 'em on your parents. Be up front, say what you think and try to work things out in advance. You may persuade them to see things your way. You may not. Sulking isn't going to convince already dubious parents that you're ready to be treated like the mature creature you are. Might also think about which exploits or thoughts are better left unsaid before you head home. Shock value can be overrated.

Look at it from your parents' point of view. They haven't changed. You have. You *know* that must throw them for a loop. Why not try to be gentle?

Younger siblings at home? They may be thinking that since they've had to clear the table for the last couple months, it's your turn for the duration of your stay. Or perhaps your parents are assuming that you'll play by the rules for the benefit of the home team, not giving your 13-year-old sister any room to whine for a later curfew. Again, just be aware of the disconcerting effect your new, grown-up self can be.

Try something obvious. If all else fails and you need a really blatant tactic, how about leaving a copy of this book open to this chapter in some obvious home spot? Highlight points you want your parents to *accidentally* stumble across. Hey, it can't hurt.

••••••••••••••••••••••••••••••••

Skip the Tarot Cards: a Better Approach to Finding Your College

There are small truckloads worth of books dedicated to the topic of how to choose the right college. Whether you're a high school student looking forward or a dissatisfied college student thinking of transferring, these books contain some helpful information. Check them out.

Since the other books pretty much have that niche well covered, this chapter is dedicated to a different variation on the theme. Namely, the all-important question of "how did I get here." As these young women look back on their college selection without the emotional tempests brought on by the May First (National Commit-Yourself-To-A-College Day) deadline, some surprising insights emerged.

C.E.O. OF Y.O.U.

Choosing a college is a voyage of self-discovery – a trip for which you are solidly at the helm. Congratulations, you are hereby dubbed the executive director of your college search. Your directive is two-fold: look inside yourself to determine who you are and what you need, then look at the schools to find a good match. The better you look inside, the more positioned you will be to make a solid choice. Note that is a *solid* choice, not the *perfect* choice. Not to shatter any illusions you may be harboring, but it may be incredibly reassuring to know that there is no one single perfect choice for any college-bound student. There are going to be a great many acceptable, if not downright great, destinations.

Here's the good news: As executive director of your college search, you take the lead in deciding where to apply and where to enroll. Sure, the colleges get to roll the dice when it comes to determining your final contenders, but don't let yourself feel as if they're playing craps with your entire future. You get to make the final choice.

Of course, you do have your very own board of directors. At the top of the power structure are your parents, or whomever is signing the tuition checks. No matter what, college is a big financial deal, and it is rare for college choices not to be influenced by the issue. Be sensitive, and talk openly about it. Also, parents may place votes that have an agenda, such as for colleges close to home or close to their hearts.

Then comes the rest of the board of directors – siblings, mentors, friends, counselors and any one who has a stake, real or imagined, in your education. There's the gardener, the grocery store clerk, a friend's mother, the guy behind you in French III and your sister's boyfriend. Everyone has an opinion, be it filled with good, faulty or self-serving advice. Like any good executive, you'll want to listen to your board of directors, consider their input, and then make your own decision. You, and only y-o-u, will have to live with the fallout, good or bad.

BEFORE THE THICK AND THIN ENVELOPES

The Human Element

When it comes to the single most important aspect when picking a school, it all boils down to one thing – the people. The young women interviewed were practically unanimous and quite vocal on this point. Indeed, for those who were unhappy and transferred, dissatisfaction with their fellow schoolmates ranked first on or near the top of their list of reasons. Here are some of their thoughts and voices.

For **Karen,** social relationships are the cornerstone of her happiness at school. She wanted *"diverse and interesting students. Meeting students is probably the most important in deciding where to apply and where to go."* Her advice was the strongest: *"Think about the type of students you want to be around and look at colleges that you think have those students."*

For **Joanne,** *"I wanted a specific demographic of students [who were] wholesome and down to earth."*

Lisa's wise words: *"Most of what you learn isn't in the classroom. It's learning about yourself and learning about others. College is more about people."*

Jane emphasized, *"The issue is not where you go to college, but what the people are like."*

Ayla transferred after her freshman year so she looked at colleges not once but twice. Here is her input. *"When you think about a college and the people, look around. I believe you should not only look for people who are like you but also people who are different from you. It's nice to be surrounded by people who you can relate to. If you decide not to change, you'll have plenty of company. You can also get to know people who are different, then pick and choose how you want to change and grow. There will be whole new groups and types of friends."*

Culture Comfort

First, know thyself. Or at least, try to get some insight into what setting you want now and make a stab at guessing what will make you happy for the next four years. Of course, this isn't going to be easy. (Think of all those self-help books that would go unsold if it were!) In what kind of environment do you thrive? What makes you comfortable? Intimate and nurturing? Wildly diverse and bustling?

The need for social interaction and sense of belonging are universal, but the specific environment that students desire are as unique as fingerprints. Fortunately, environment is just where colleges differ enormously. It is actually quite easy to see the differences among colleges' architecture and the curriculum, but it is the differences in that intangible *vibe* that makes each campus distinct. That vibe comes from the students and their interactions. It's harder to research this than, say, the college's average SAT scores, but no less critical.

> **"**
> *I wanted a specific demographic of students [who were] wholesome and down to earth.*
> **"**
> JOANNE

Simone chose her university for its *"liberal, progressive and passionate attitudes."* Coming from a liberal background, she was comfortable with the political and social views on campus, including the acceptance of the very visible gay community and the fact that condoms were freely distributed around campus.

Analytical and down to earth in her selection process, **Anne B.'s** primary needs were straightforward: *"a supportive environment, not too much drinking and clean bathrooms!"* Anne ended up at an all-women's college. Does she miss guys? Yes. Is she happy? Absolutely!

Charlotte wanted to be a part of a liberal atmosphere with students to match. When she visited her university's campus, the first student Charlotte met had purple hair. The purple hair became a symbol of the school's general mindset and exactly what Charlotte was looking for. She began to feel very positively toward the school and after a thorough and more objective review of the school, she enrolled.

Leslie chose her college for its ideals; a *"liberal outlook, how they approach learning, what is the purpose of being there. I still believe in learning for loving to learn."* She also made her selection based on its reputation (and her observation) as *"laid back,"* more in keeping with her personality.

Ann hoped to burst out of the limited social scene at her exclusive but sheltered high school with the proper college choice. *"When I visited [my college], it was just what I imagined college to be like. Very historic. Academically it was fantastic. The students I talked to loved it there. While there were snobby, rich kids, they all said there were tons of really cool kids. You only need a few really good friends to be happy."*

The Reality of Money

Except for a very lucky few, school costs will be a key element in school decisions. Frankly, how could it not with the price tag for a diploma from many private universities and colleges across the country tipping into the six-figure bracket? Calmly and rationally talking about college costs with parents may be the most adult thing many college-bound young adults have to do. It can be a hard discussion, especially if you've slaved away to get into the *crème de la crème* of Ivy Leagues only to discover that the money isn't really there to send you to your dream. It can be hard to look beyond yourself and see how that much money will affect your parents and your siblings. So if the prospect of attending your dream school evaporates due to cost, you certainly won't be the first student to deal with this. The money issue is real. Face it and move on. Believe it or not, you may just end up at a school that you like better. Regardless you're going to be fine and get a great education.

Walking away from a high-priced school, **Lindsay** instead chose a school with a great reputation that was also affordable. It turned out to be a fantastic choice. Her school provided *"the ultimate college experience, strong academics, great sports teams and a fun college town."*

Money played a key role in **Charlotte's** decision as well. From the beginning of her search process, Charlotte sought schools with great art programs, thinking she would double major in art history and studio art. When acceptance letters started rolling in, Charlotte evaluated the various art programs, curricula and locations – but also let the financial aid package help her make the final decision. Again, the decision proved to be a good match. She had a blast with her college experience.

Does Size Matter?

The answer is usually yes. The universal description that the right school has a good fit may be a bit overused, but for good reason. Finding the best university for you is a lot like finding a dress that you love. It needs to reflect your personal style and make you feel great. And just like clothing, a preference emerges somewhere along the line – and size is a critical element! So think it through ahead of time. Big university vs. small liberal arts college. Huge lecture halls vs. intimate seminars. Just remember that it is totally *your* choice. Don't let other people impose their preferences on you. It never works when shopping for clothes, does it?

When **Kate** visited colleges she came to realize that attending a very large school was important to her. At one small, top-rated liberal arts college she uneasily felt as if the students were high school kids trying to be college students.

As the process continued, Kate came to realize that after attending school with some of the same classmates for 13 years, she was also seeking anonymity. Kate wanted a campus where she could shed her old high school self.

The perfect resolution for Kate, as it turned out, was a university with a residential college system. (By the way, this type of system – a university organized into smaller living groups that make the school feel more personable – was popular among many of the women interviewed. However, a few did feel confined in the smaller setting.) Kate ended up loving the instant socialization that the residential colleges provided.

> " *...when I get to upper-level classes, they'll be smaller, much smaller.* "
>
> SYDNEY

When it comes to class size ... surprise surprise ... freshman are more often than not piled into large freshman intro classes and seminars. This holds true of the most elite and even very small schools. Ask if this matters to you, and as always do some research. Are the 300-person lectures broken down into weekly discussion groups or labs with T.A.s so you get person contact and assistance? (FYI – The young women interviewed generally gave high marks for these arrangements.) Do the classes get substantially smaller the more advanced the courses?

Like many incoming freshmen, **Sydney** *"had heard about the huge freshman seminar classes. One had about 500 students in it! In the end, I let the people influence me. I had heard there were a lot of interesting people in my desired program and decided that would be more important than class size. Besides, when I get to upper-level classes, they'll be smaller, much smaller."*

AFTER YOU'VE STOPPED HAUNTING THE MAILBOX

Take A Lo-o-o-ong Look

OK. You've got the thick envelopes filled with flattering acceptance letters and exciting class schedules clutched tightly in your hand. You've got a couple tempting options. The next step is some very important advice: Take a good look at your top choices. A very good lo-o-o-ong look. Then look again. This may be where you spend the next four years of your life, and you want them to be good ones.

Acceptances come out the end of March through the middle of April, and decisions are just about always due May first. You could have as little as two weeks to make your final choice. So plan ahead. Don't think of Spring Break as a recreational event this year, but as college countdown time.

The nice thing about this stage of the college process is that once you're admitted, you're a hot commodity. The colleges want you, and will more than likely bend over backwards to accommodate your requests. So go make it happen. Call the admissions office and see what they can do for you. If you can, go visit. Move past the standard campus tour and information session. Sit in on classes and meet with students. Brave the cafeteria and check out the local coffeehouses. Try to absorb each college's general personality.

Sydney had the right idea. After the letters came out she spent plenty of time poking about on the three campuses where she knew she was interested. Her final visits made her final choice a clear-cut decision. *"I spent three to four days on each campus, getting to know* *students, classes and the general feeling of each school."*

(Re)Visit the campus

During **Arielle's** final campus visit, she browsed through the bookstore and loved the discovery that Medieval Studies were offered on the curriculum – even though she was interested in majoring in Molecular Biology. *"Sometimes the tiniest thing can turn your head. Visit the school before choosing it; be open to new ideas."*

Leslie advised trying to find a friend on your prospective campus to whom you can talk honestly. *"Knowing and talking to [old friends from high school] was more effective than simply visiting and spending the night with a stranger."*

Go to an Event, Any Event

When you visit your soon-to-be-maybe college, go to whatever events are offered during your stay. Dance concert or basketball game, it doesn't matter. The audience will be the main attraction for you. What are the people like?

Check Out the Bulletin Boards

Take a moment to read about what is happening on campus on the bulletin boards. See anything interesting?

Check Out the Campus Publications

Browse through whatever campus publications you can get your hands on, but especially seek out the student-produced newspaper. What's on the front page? Insightful articles on campus issues? Boring hard-news rehashes? Party announcements? Make sure to check out the opinion page (get the real scoop on the campus's heartbeat) and the classifieds. Do you like what you see?

Scarlett's favorite research tool for colleges was their newspapers. First she perused the various papers via the school Web sites, then zeroed in on the op-ed pages. She felt that they best reflected the intellectual life of the school.

> **"**
> *Sometimes*
> *the tiniest thing*
> *can turn*
> *your head...*
> *be open*
> *to new ideas.*
> **"**
> ARIELLE

Tour Guides

If you've got the time, you may want to consider taking a second tour of the school to get a final look. This time, take a careful look at the tour guide. Sure, it's just one person, but this one person is a direct representative of the admissions office. If your tour guide is way off the mark in terms of your-kinda-folks…keep looking around. This could be a bad omen.

Graduate Students? Yes or No?

Conventional wisdom claims that too many graduate students means that the undergrads are ignored. Not necessarily. Graduate students can be great teachers and mentors, and add a certain stability to a campus. This is one of those factors that is entirely up to you and your preferences. Just think it through ahead of time.

Computers

After visiting Web sites of the schools where students were interviewed, it became apparent that the quality of the sites varied enormously. A college or university that isn't computer literate is possibly or probably not going to be able to teach those skills to you. This is a wired world, after all. Make sure that what is being offered and used is what you are going to need in your life.

(Re)Visit the U.S. News and World Report Web site

Now that you're down to a few choices, check out the Web site for U.S. News and World Report, again. Check out how your top choices rank in their index. The site does a good job of quantifying the objective aspects of the colleges you are considering, such as class sizes and male-female student ratios. **Kate** liked the site especially because it provided links to the schools' Web pages.

Know however, that these rankings are the stuff of controversy. There is an army of educators who find this Web site the work of the devil. Things get sticky when the report tries to quantify more subjective data. Academic reputation for example. Touchy! But figure out what matters to you, and see if U.S. News and World Report can help you.

While you're at it you might just take the College Personality Test on the same Web site. It is handy as a quick-sort for your college likes and dislikes. It asks subjective questions and gives you quick feedback. If your college counselor seems, shall we say, out of touch, this little quiz might be especially helpful.

Academics: Lest We Forget

Somewhere along the line, visit classes. This is especially important when you're making your final choice. So go hit one of your favorite subjects and see what they've got. Think of your adored high school classes (say, History), and go sample a History of the Tudor Period or South American Revolutions class. Peek into its academic cousin, Political Science, then head down the hall for a microbiology lecture, if that's your game.

Regardless of whatever turns you on, just go see as much as possible. Try to sit in on both a huge intro class as well as a cozy upper-division seminar to get a sense of what your classroom experience will be like throughout all your years there. It's time truly well invested. And just in case you feel self-conscious – don't. Profs and students are used to visitors. In fact, you'll probably see other prospective students just like yourself lurking in the back.

What About Your Major?

Just how much should you think about what courses will be offered? If you're dead set on a certain major from Day One, you'll probably want to seek out the best-college-for-you in that major. If you're like the majority of students and have an idea but aren't sure, think about these stories. Also, remember that college is about intellectual growth and discovery. Many students stumble upon a field they never knew existed, fall in love with it, and happily pursue the major. So try to avoid tunnel vision.

Joanne decided, *"I wanted to be a doctor."* Knowing she would eventually attend medical school helped narrow the field. She first sought the appropriate curriculum, then the type of students she wanted on the journey with her.

Even though she knew that she wanted a career in the field of psychology or psychiatry, **Anne B.** didn't worry about choosing a school based on her prospective major. She was more concerned with the excellence of the school itself, which – since her grades and board scores were very strong – was a given. She was happy with her selection.

> **"**
> *It's not enough to assume that since there are a lot of students on campus, you'll just have fun.*
> **"**
> HOLDEN

One little wrinkle to think about. During the decision-making process, **Charlotte** found certain classes that she wanted to take and professors whose classes she wanted. With dismay, Charlotte found that teachers sometimes take sabbaticals. With them can go their much anticipated classes.

Where is This Place?

Are you a city mouse or county mouse? If you're in a city, can you escape to the country when you need a break? And vice versa? This is the time to really think about where the college is located and what the implications are. Will it take two trains and a bus to get home from what feels to be the University of Pluto, or will your parents be able to knock on your door with a surprise visit after a 15-minute drive? And which option feels comfortable to you?

Holden cautions, *"Be really sure you understand what location means. Large city, small community environs are considerations. You can't possibly know until you're in the school if the college-planned activities are enough to satisfy you. I love to go to clubs and museums. It's not enough to assume that since there are a lot of students on campus, you'll just have fun."*

What about the University's Wallet?

What does diversity mean to you? Ethnic diversity is pretty easy to categorize. Look for what you want. Prospective colleges can and will readily present statistics. Financial diversity, however, is a more subtle delineator. Here are two takes on the issue of money – its presence and lack thereof.

After hearing about the abundance of scholarships, **Scarlett** had anticipated more variety in her peers, specifically financial diversity. It astonished her to find *"the similarity between the students in terms of study habits and social skills. I was surprised by the lack of lower-income students."*

Coming from a private school, **Leslie** had lived with financial abundance most of her life. Like Scarlett, she too expected more diversity in college. What emerged at her school was wealth for some and great need for others. *"There are a lot of really wealthy kids, the contrast can be uncomfortable."*

Brand Name Fever

Just like brand-name clothes, a brand-name school is one with a certain cachet in the eye of the beholder. It's so easy to get caught up on the brand name itself, regardless of what reality lies beneath or what other options exist. School counselors, parents and classmates often walk, talk, and dream brand-name colleges. It's every advertiser's and PR person's goal, the creation of an "I gotta have it" option. Honestly, it can be hard *not* to topple into the seductive spell and historical prestige of a brand-name school.

Here, as food for thought, is how two young women saw the choice.

Simone's search for college was initially fueled by her attraction to brand names, and she admitted she relied too much on that. But as she reviewed the schools on her list, they were either too conservative or too hip or too close to home. Perhaps she mused, she should have tried to be more introspective about what school was right for her. Yes, she took the brand-name option. Was she happy? Yes!

Holden, having turned down one brand name (a bigger brand name) for yet another brand-name school said, *"You don't have to go to the best school you get into."* There was a reason here. The idea was to go where you would be happiest and learn and connect the most. Holden had only a few regrets, including the fact that she didn't go back to her alternate-choice school for one last look around. But was she happy? Yes!

"Them" or How Family and Peer Pressure Fits In

While you may be working under the impression that *you* are the one going to college, and chances are you have passed your eighteenth birthday and therefore are legally an adult, you may discover that family members are heavily invested (and this does not only mean financially) in your future. Friends have their own agendas as well. Everyone's got an opinion, and of course everyone thinks that their opinion is the most valid. This influence can be overwhelming. It can also be particularly convincing if they, in the case of your parents or grandparents, are footing the bill. The trick is to negotiate a balance between listening to yourself and gleaning the bits of good advice that trickle your way.

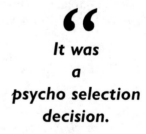

It was
a
psycho selection
decision.

ALEXANDRA

Jeni's family was *involved* at the large private university where her brother attended. This made the notion of Jeni's attendance a *fait à complis*, so she applied for early admission. Surprise. Denied. *"My feeling was of relief that I didn't get into my early admission school. At the time, I really didn't know where I wanted to go and in the end did not even apply there again for Spring consideration."*

Jeni simply didn't like the school. Throughout her life she did *everything* her brother did and wanted a different experience. It would have been too comfortable, too easy to take this path…it was a gift she didn't want to accept.

GO WITH YOUR GUT

Of all the advice flung your way, this may sound too nonscientific and touchy-feely. However, it's also dead-on. Gut feelings are based on a multitude of factors, all carefully weighed and processed internally. "Going with your gut" is personal, indescribable, and delicious when it just plain feels right. It is very frequently the deciding factor.

Meredith cleared the cobwebs and looked inside. *"I ended up ignoring what everyone told me to do and went where I felt right. I'm very happy."* And, further, she advised, *"Apply where you feel comfortable; listen to your parents' advice; don't be discouraged if people tell you you won't get in."*

Harriet also emphasized *"… go with your gut feeling; do not pay too much attention to things like the prestige of a school, etc. Go where you feel comfortable and think you'd have fun academically and socially."*

Sophie courageously selected a college far from home. This was in spite of the fact that during her middle school years she had agreed to sleep-away camp two summers then bolted home early, not once, but twice! Sophie did rely on her prep-school counselor, but was most influenced and *"learned a lot about [her] school from just walking around the campus."* Sophie's advice: *"Follow your own feelings. If you walk onto a campus and just FEEL like you belong there, that's a good place for you."*

For **Alexandra** *"It was a psycho selection decision."* She covered the map in her decision process. Warm climate to cold; small to extra-large; new experience to a parent's alma mater. Her open mind freed the process to appraise all possibilities. In the end she decided *"I don't think it's necessary to visit or sleep over. The college tour can be a positive or a negative - a fluke."* In the end, it was her gut that led her to her decision.

Putting it all in perspective, **Alison** admitted, *"…the people, they all looked like me."*

Not the End of the World

Take a deep breath. You're not dealing with the end of the world here. The bottom line is that – believe it or not – there is more than one "right" choice here.

Yes, choosing a college is a Big Deal, probably the most significant decision in which you've been personally involved. But let's keep it all in perspective: There are students who never get a choice, and some bright, qualified kids who by accident of birth never make it past the eighth grade or get any schooling at all. With that said, here are some thoughts to start with, seen by collegiate veterans.

Anne B. found the selection process difficult. Slowly she realized that what she wanted didn't exist. Her advice: *"Don't make the assumption of the perfect school. These schools came along 100 years ago; I came along a lot later."*

Lindsay was one of the many young women who agreed that while she was thrilled with her college choice, she would have been happy at another school (or schools) as well. It is a big world out there. One or more rejection letters aren't going to ruin your chances in life.

Lauren came to a similar realization: *"There's not only one right school. You can transfer. It takes time (different amounts of time for everyone) to adjust."*

Even **Simone**, who was driven to attend a brand-name school, came to muse that if she had attended less of a powerhouse school, she probably would have been just as satisfied with her education.

Handling Rejection

It's possible that you'll be rejected by your first-choice college. Yup, it happens and it could happen to you. Do what you need to do to accept that fact, let that dream drift away, and move on! Hold a ceremony and burn your rejection letters. Maybe shred 'em. Or shred 'em and then burn 'em. Just don't worry. There are plenty of great schools. One will open its arms.

> **Don't make the assumption of the perfect school. These schools came along 100 years ago.**
>
> ANNE B.

The Ultimate Selection Method

For **Lauren**, it became a matter then of choosing between a very large, excellent, public school not too far from home, and two others, both excellent, both private and vastly more expensive. Family members put in their own in two cents. Teachers tried to influence her. Ultimately, her grandparents agreed to make up the dollar difference between public and private. Finding the decision difficult, she wrote down pros and cons of two of the schools and in the end, unable to come to a decision, she tossed a coin...really.

● ●

ON THE FAST TRACK TO MAKING A DECISION?

Sure you are. This is the big one. Stop first and make a list. Get the big picture. Make sure these questions, common sense and otherwise, get answered. The answers can make all the difference.

Think! What was great about high school? What do you want to change? Make your college selection accordingly.

You are in charge. This is probably your first big decision. And it is yours, you know. Why not try to do the best you can? You will also reap the rewards.

How are the people? Highly important. Talk to them. Do they look like folks with whom you would want to be friends? Check it all out.

What is the community like? Happy-go-lucky? Nerdy? Artsy? Intense? And is it a match for you? Ask yourself the important questions from here and elsewhere and the answer will emerge.

Can you and yours afford it? Don't be squeamish on this one. It's a big part of the decision for many families. Get it out now, not later. Why wait?

Visit the campus even if you went there before. Do this! If you're serious about this institution after acceptance letters arrive, visit again for a longer duration; say three to four days. Visit classes. People-watch. Hopefully, visit during weather you think you might hate. And while you are at it, drop the schools you are just not interested in. Don't waste your time even if their pleas and responses are rather convincing and attractive. Too distracting.

Size. Too large, too confining, or just right? Class size make sense?

Check out this school on the Web. Is the Web site up to snuff? How about student Web pages? What kinds of folks are there? No student Web pages? Is that a good sign? Look up the student newspaper in the school Web site. No school newspaper on the Internet? Not a good sign. Is this school ready for the new millennium?

U.S. News and World report Web site. Give this another once-over.

Academics. How are the classes you visited? Exciting or dull? Suit you? That's what matters.

Location and distance. Check out the neighboring town(s). Too close, too far or just right?

Brand name. Important? Or not?

Respect your gut reaction. Tummy comfort. It will be serving you throughout your life. Let it sprout during your college search.

First-choice school sent a very thin, no-thank-you letter? Sometimes these letters are more of a gift than they appear at first.

Not to worry. There are great schools out there, and many will be a good fit for you.

• •

HOLDEN'S STORY: WHEN YOU EXCEL IN SPORTS

After years of incredibly hard work developing soccer, volleyball or gymnastics skills, what if collegiate coaches and recruiters put you on their short list? Lucky you. Like several of the young women interviewed, you could find yourself wooed by a panoply of colleges. Free trips out to visit, choice dorm rooms dangled, possibly scholarship offers. This obviously can dramatically change the college selection process. But some universal truths on smart selection still apply, and hidden downsides lurk as well.

This is **Holden's** story.

First came the whirlwind.

Volleyball took Holden down a different track than most college applicants. Top-tier schools were interested in her thanks to her reputation as a volleyball whiz and a star on her prep school and club teams. National meets, which attract college coaches and recruiters, showcased her talents.

Then the frenzy began. Scouts and coaches launched a heavy press to persuade Holden to commit early to their particular schools. Dazzled by offers of special weekends and all-expense-paid trips to various campuses, she felt flattered and overwhelmed, pleased and protective of her life and the budgets of these schools.

Holden had a busy high school schedule over and above volleyball. She was serious about maintaining strong grades, and she was a principal dancer in her prep school's dance company. The annual dance concert, which required countless hours of rehearsal, was scheduled right around the time of the recruiting trips. Without the time to visit every school wooing her, Holden decided that she could not accept all these trips in good faith. When she toured schools early on in the selection process, Holden sometimes forewent the organized tour. In retrospect, she'd probably do things differently. *"I set up meetings with volleyball coaches while on campuses. I have mixed feelings about that. Good thing to do if you have the time, but don't sacrifice the tour or the [chance to] attend classes [in session]."*

Next came the pressure.

The schools actively recruiting Holden not surprisingly wanted her to commit months before the April first letters were mailed. She bought into the pressure, feeling at one point that she would lose an admission offer entirely if she didn't commit to a school early. Suddenly those missed visits meant that she was making a huge decision without full information.

Looking back, Holden realized that perhaps the dance concert wasn't all that important. Perhaps she could have missed a few days of school, especially since she was in good academic standing. Perhaps it would have been wiser to at least check out all the offers, experience the campus life offered to her, and get to know the volleyball team members. Most importantly, when it came down to her two favorite schools, she said, *"I should have made time to visit both."*

Holden never knew if she made the wrong choice. While she's exceedingly happy at her university, she had lingering regret about not exploring all her options. She also regretted rejecting the idea of attending one parent's alma mater, simply on the gut feeling that she didn't want to follow in his footsteps. She admitted, *"If I had kept an open mind, I probably would have enjoyed myself there."*

The good, the bad, the reality.

To Holden, one of the great advantages of being a college athlete was arriving at campus two weeks before school started. Her time was filled with team bonding activities, fitness training and acclimation to the city, but she wished that she could have attended the all-school orientation as well. She wanted the best of both worlds.

Unfortunately, her athletic commitment prevented her from participating in the school's general orientation – meaning she lost an important chance to make new friends. While she was able to meet 15 or so fellow athletes, many of them sophomores and upperclassmen, the non-sports freshmen had literally dozens of friends by the time classes started. One advantage of getting to know the older team members, though, was learning how to best cope with the administrative bureaucracy and get what she wanted with minimal headaches. On the other hand, she never knew what a university-planned week of orientation might have brought. *"I had a picture in my mind what it [school] was going to be like, and when it wasn't that at first. I was disappointed. I just needed time to settle in."*

The volleyball was satisfying. She adored this component of her education, even though it was highly demanding. She had the chance to see friends from her high school volleyball circuit when playing other college teams. However, she also learned that no matter how glowing the recruiting promises or stellar a player's high school athletic accomplishments, not all freshmen get to play their first year. While Holden didn't cope with this personally, many of her friends had to deal with the heartache that can bring.

While Holden had a large group of friends outside volleyball, she felt the sport had placed her with a group of young women with whom she might not have been friends otherwise. She believed this was a benefit of teamwork. Her school also provided peer counseling, so Holden relies on her assigned upperclassmen to keep her abreast of dates for guest speakers, where to find late night snacks, and which were the best professors. The assigned mentors became her constant e-mail buddies and good friends.

Just half way through her first year, Holden already felt pressure to play for four years. She however was not obligated by a scholarship, which gave her latitude. Her decision to play or not will be her personal choice alone. Junior year abroad enticed Holden, which meant that if she chose that path, her decision to stop playing volleyball would be a done deal.

• •

LEILA'S STORY: SHE CAME, SHE SAW, SHE LEFT

Leila made sure that her prep school readied her for the best of colleges, cramming her schedule with AP classes and studying hard. After all, it was simply accepted at her high school and among her close friends that they would attend the most prestigious school that accepted them. No one, including Leila, questioned this path.

Leila had known for what felt like ages that she wanted to attend a college located in a mid-sized town no more than one hour away from a major city. The academics would be top-notch, of course, as would be the parties, guys and social life. Beyond that, however, she didn't have a specific focus. She wasn't an athlete, nor did she consider herself a musician (despite 11 years of piano lessons), nor was she passionate about a single area of study. Zeroing in on schools that intrigued her felt like a rather arbitrary endeavor. She was seriously burnt out from plowing through high school, and her decisions regarding where to apply were disjointed and unfocused. Worse, Leila abandoned her early preferences along the wayside.

Then the responses started rolling in. Her first-choice university rejected her, then a second one. Leila's choice came down to two comparably sized institutions, one isolated and one in the middle of a bustling city. The university she chose – with her father's guidance, and where her mother had attended medical school – was located in a tiny, isolated town. In other words, she chose the opposite of her dream college. Right away Leila knew that she had made a dreadful mistake. She had come to her college decision for all the wrong reasons.

"I do not think I applied to the right schools in the first place in many cases. I hung out with a very smart group of popular girls and they were going back East and Ivy, or it was 'in' to go back East. I had family there and thought it was the right choice to make. I disregarded many schools from the college pool. Also I was burnt out from high school and by the time I applied, I just wanted it to be over. If you know someone attending [a particular school], go out with them, get a sense of the social setting. If you are from the West, go during WINTER.

I always thought 'if unsure, go with the best,' but this is not good advice in retrospect. Friends went to good schools, so I wanted to go to a good school."

How Leila Made Her Selection	How She Wished She Had
1. Brand name	1. Environment of city
2. First choice rejected her	2. Location
3. Self-inflicted pressure to attend best school possible.	3. Size of city/town
4. Indirect pressure from parents	4. Size of university
5. Interviewer	5. Curriculum
6. Parent's alma mater	6. Self-inflicted pressure to attend best school possible
7. Nice weather on day of visit	7. Check out WINTER weather

The realities of school never improved for Leila. The pervasive Greek system (over 30% participation), which seemed to be just another fact of college life when she checked out the school initially, turned out to be something she absolutely hated for many reasons. (Reread the Greek chapter for a full rundown.)

She made up her mind to bail.

However, encouraged to tough it out until June, Leila floated along. She felt a little bit better knowing that she would be sprung soon, but still *"felt like a stranger walking around…frustrated because I envisioned the college experience as being different. I was most frightened when… I got really sick for the first time. I would feel lonely and isolated and…hated feeling like a whiner."*

Then came a brutal discovery: Leila wouldn't be admitted to the university of her choice until she had completed her sophomore year. She could either stick it out in her current unhappy situation or head to a community junior college, which was personally hard for her to swallow coming from her elite school. Faced with that option, she sucked up her pride and headed to a community college for a year.

To Leila's surprise, her sophomore year turned out to be a welcome experience. She discovered she was not necessarily smarter than the other students, but simply well prepared to study effectively. She excelled in her classes and found the professors enthusiastic and very accomplished. Leila also discovered that the wide variety of students (age, disciplines, socioeconomic standing) brought richness and texture to the class discussions. In short, she had a very good year.

When Leila returned to university life in her junior year, she landed at a large university in a big city. Greek life was a much smaller aspect of the school (only 10% participation), one that she could easily avoid. Leila – an upper classman and surrounded by students studying her discipline (Cultural Anthropology) – had many friends who she saw often, and had the confidence to approach her T.A.s and professors to get the same kind of personal contact she would have had handed to her at a smaller school.

Leila bore some regret that her original college dream, which included staying at the same place except for a junior year abroad, were not realized. However, she enjoyed a rich intellectual and social life, and possessed a mature optimism that life was turning out just right.

"It is not where you go, but what you make of it. I probably should have become more involved in events at [my original school] so that I did not dwell on my unhappiness."

In the end, Leila's words of advice were. *"Go with your gut."*

• •

What Ever Happened to Happily Ever After?

Welcome to the collegiate myth of Happily Ever After. Throughout high school there is a huge build-up surrounding the college selection process. After years of hard work the acceptance letters come in, your agreement to enroll is excitedly sent out, and the angels sing….right?

Er, not necessarily. Fairy tales tend to be fractured in real life. Think more the Brothers Grimm than perfection. Although the vast majority of incoming freshmen are content (or grow to be content) with their college choices, the glorious university you selected may actually prove to be a toad. Or you may feel like the pre-prince Cinderella in a world of stepsisters. Something is critically out of sync. The key question, then, is the mismatch temporary or terminal? Are the problems stemming from within you? Are the problems with the school something you can take steps to resolve? Or is time to fold your hand and get out of town?

There is a lot of soul-searching involved in answering these questions, and it ain't easy. But it is important to recognize whether the dissatisfaction comes from a specific professor, roommate or noisy neighbor or from the whole darn place. Think about whether that gut-wrenching sense of not belonging comes from high school separation pain, from holing up in your room like a hermit, from a university population following a truly different drummer, or from something so deep within you it's impossible to outrun.

For whatever reason, most college counselors treat the issue of a transfer like an eight-letter word. It's whispered about, rarely directly acknowledged, almost as if it were a sign of failure. If you're nodding your head in secret agreement, stop it this instant. A transfer simply means that something went haywire in the college selection process. It's not a capital mistake that will haunt you the rest of your life. Indeed, a simple fix could mean the difference between a college experience you adore rather than merely survive.

This chapter will address the stories of four young women who faced the transfer question. See if any of their situations match yours.

WHAT *EXACTLY* IS THE PROBLEM?

Just as the reasons why a college fit can be wonderful are as countless and variable as personalities, so are the reasons why things go wrong. That said, however, the most common theme that emerged was a persistent feeling of not fitting in. Of being out of context. Of things not being the way they were expected to be. Do any of the following scenarios sound familiar?

Ayla had fought hard to get into her chosen university. She had been initially rejected, but mounted a well-planned and ultimately successful campaign to appeal that decision. After this much work, Ayla must have known this school inside and out. Right? Well, a mere three weeks into her freshman year, she felt as if the breath had been knocked out of her. How could such a large place offer such little diversity? Ayla felt uneasy. Pre-Med students dominated the scene, which left her feeling forlorn and excluded as she started to pursue her intended Philosophy major. What really killed her was that while the university had a top-notch Philosophy department, *"fifty percent of my major is learned outside of school. Discussions with friends and experiences with them help shape who you are."* She had anticipated lively, challenging dialogues of wildly divergent thought. Not only did these never arise, Ayla was dissatisfied by her conversations with classmates who were more linear-thinking science students.

> **"**
> **I felt like a stranger walking around.**
> **"**
> LEILA

Jane lamented the lack of socio-economic diversity at her school. She found herself disconcertingly among *"a lot of kids with a lot of money."* Even though she came from a financially stable background, she felt uncomfortable.

Abby also discovered that she felt as if she had little in common with her student body. For one, she only spent an hour a day on schoolwork her first semester, having been extraordinarily well prepared academically. Her fellow students spent the majority of their waking hours toiling away, often because – it seemed to Abby – they didn't have effective study methods. With an all-work-no-play mentality, the campus was empty and the students were invisible, locked away at their desks.

Moreover, the college was nestled in a bucolic suburb about a 40-minutes drive from a major city, but inconvenient public transportation schedules made it much longer or downright impossible to get to the city. Abby felt trapped. Apart from campus activities, there was little to do in this teeny, tiny town. Since most of the students hailed from rural communities – another surprise – they were content to stay local for their social life.

After having heard so much about the intellectual atmosphere of this renowned institution, Abby was unimpressed. *"I thought because of its reputation that I would find motivated students and incredible professors."* She felt the professors demanded rote learning – re-creating high school without her gaggle of close friends. There were no stimulating student discussions, no awareness of the outside world or even pop culture. Even how the students dressed was a throwback. Sure, the campus was absolutely beautiful, but for Abby, at its core the school was *"boring."*

Unable to discern if her unhappiness was temporary or deeply rooted in her school choice, **Sam** decided by the spring semester that transferring would solve her mounting dissatisfaction regardless. Part of the problem was the fraternity and sorority scene. Part of the problem was the homogeneity of her peers; being rich, white and vaguely elitist. Overall, she didn't like the whole feeling-tone of the place, and getting out seemed like the most viable option. In fact, getting out seemed like the only option. From Sam's point of view, anything would be a lot more fun than where she was. So out it was. Boom. She reviewed her original choices, looked at some new options and set out to decide to which college she wanted to transfer. Then she hit a major stumbling block: The universities (and other schools like them) on her list only accepted transfers after the sophomore year. But Sam was unhappy then. Right then. After a considerable amount of thought and some long talks with her parents, Sam decided to stay. Her family environment, for better or for worse, was one that *"stressed success over happiness."*

SO WHAT HAPPENED?

Although many of the issues concerning Jane, Sam, Ayla, and Abby could (and perhaps should) have raised their ugly little heads during the college selection phase, it's impossible to fully fathom the impact factors have until you're living the

> **"**
> **Don't**
> **be afraid**
> **to fix**
> **your mistakes.**
> **"**
>
> AYLA

college life 24/7. These women found that retrospection was illuminating. You can benefit from the women's belated realizations and spare yourself the first-hand regret.

With a lot of encouragement from her high school counselors, **Abby** had chosen to attend a highly ranked school that was the *"best"* that accepted her. *"I saw everyone around me only applying to top-notch schools."* She was under substantial pressure from her prep school and parents to do the same. *"I essentially applied to the same selective schools as everyone else in my senior class because those were the schools we were told to consider. And they were the only 'acceptable' schools."* Then when she got into her college of choice, she figured that given its reputation it *had* to be the right choice. She felt lucky, and didn't think about it any more. *"After all, this school ranked very high nationally, so once accepted, how could I turn it down? I thought I would love the school, but I really hated it."* Looking back to how she tackled her school search, Abby regrettably realized that *"it didn't seem to matter what I did before or even after I was admitted, because my mind already seemed made up. Even though I was dissatisfied with what I saw after I was admitted, I dismissed the criticisms [that came my way]."*

Jane similarly fell under the spell of her chosen school's brand name. But she also was captivated by the rather romantic idea of attending college in a big Eastern city. Once that thought was firmly lodged in her head, other criteria were pretty much ignored. Not surprisingly, Jane quickly realized that she may have made a mistake. In fact, there were signs at the June orientation that her college didn't represent a good fit. The orientation was filled with a tight schedule and curfews – a rigid structure she didn't even have to endure in high school. Things didn't improve in the fall. *"It was always told to me, 'when your parents leave your dorm room, you feel the greatest feeling of freedom.' I kept waiting for that feeling, but it never came."*

In contrast, **Ayla** *thought* she had thoroughly researched her school beyond its brand name. It had pretty much everything she wanted: a great Philosophy department, a beach nearby so she could continue surfing, a broad range of great opportunities (like a pottery class from a world-renowned artist that she was able to take in her first semester), and a comparatively reasonable price tag. But was it a dream come true? Not in the least. *"I had a funny feeling at first sight, but I thought I was just nervous like everyone else."* Unfortunately, that feeling didn't go away. Sometimes all the research in the world can't protect you from a decision that simply turns out to be wrong.

MAYBE IT'S NOT YOU

Sometimes a few of the factors that led you to your current unhappy situation are not your fault. Perhaps unexpectedly, choosing a college can be a case of buyer beware. It's easy to forget that at the core, colleges work overtime to sell themselves in the best possible light. Occasionally, that line between salesmanship and misrepresentation is crossed.

So mystified by her reaction to the college, **Abby** went back to review the school's view book to see where things had gone wrong. To her surprise, Abby felt that the view book was downright misleading. The campus had a fabulous social scene. Wrong! To Abby's standard, there was no social life at all. It was easy to get to the city. Wrong! Unless hours on multiple busses which stopped running at 10:00 p.m. counted.

FOR THE RECORD

Anne B. – who was a year behind Abby at the same prep school – attended Abby's original college. Both girls came from similar religious and family backgrounds. **But whereas Abby found disaster, Anne B. was absolutely delighted with her college choice.** She especially loved many of the very experiences that Abby so loathed, such as the quiet, small-town atmosphere.

While these examples are subjective calls, Abby believed that she found factually incorrect material in the view book as well. The school's published retention rate (a good measure of student satisfaction which tracks how many freshmen came back for the second year) was factually incorrect. It claimed a 96% retention rate, when in fact Abby was among a group of seven evacuees who decamped to the same new college. With about 500 in her freshman class, that meant that the retention rate hovered actually around 85%. Abby wondered how many more in her class left for other universities as well, driving the retention rate even lower.

In retrospect, Abby also felt she talked to the wrong students when doing her research. She spent her on-campus time with Danielle, a fellow graduate of Abby's prep school. While at the time they seemed to share similar philosophies, Abby realized how different they were. What Danielle liked, Abby didn't.

SIGNIFICANT ADVICE

More than once in this survey, college view books proved to be misleading or downright inaccurate. As a common marketing tool, they also tended to be filled with rose-tinted hyperbole. Be aware of this, and double-check the aspects of a college that are important to you.

THERE'S ALWAYS PLAN 'B'

Of the four women mentioned in this chapter, three chose to leave. After considering the option seriously, Sam decided to remain at her school and in the end and was happy with her decision. Jane ended up coming home for a year, then entered a different college within her original university. For Ayla and Abby, transferring to different schools proved to be the key to collegiate Happily Ever After.

Ayla found her new school satisfying and fun. *"I would love to stay in college forever."* In fact, *"The only change I'd make on campus would be more classes, more often."* The town is idyllic. *"It's a special place in the world."* Her words of advice for others who may find themselves in similar situations were to *"follow your dreams and you can't go wrong. Don't be afraid to fix your mistakes. It will be worth it."*

Abby's move to a large private university provided a fantastic diversity of ideas and passion for school, work and causes. Abby discovered lively student groups, intellectually stimulating classes, and casual debates that never died down. Challenged intellectually and fulfilled socially, Abby was happier than she could ever imagine. With 20/20 hindsight, she advised: *"Consider all of your options and don't be blinded by the prestige of a school. It's not the most important thing."*

Jane's hard-earned words of wisdom were to *"follow your own instincts; you have that luxury. High school never prepares you."*

• •

FIGHT OR FLIGHT?

Take your time in pursuing this overview. It's important to sit back and really think about the situation in which you've landed. Try to come up with a realistic take on just what happened, and then a realistic plan of action. Remember too, no need to go through this alone. Bounce ideas off of your favorite friends, family and school counselors. That's what they're there for.

Are you sure there's a problem? This is flat-out the hardest question, which only you can answer. Have you landed in absolutely the wrong place for you, or are you dealing with temporary hardships that will improve if you give it time and invest some energy? The transition to college can be incredibly tough, granted. But pause to think. Is this a temporary case of homesickness? Of feeling that you don't belong? Are potential friends out there, but are you dorm-bound and afraid to seek them? Have you honestly explored and experienced your college? Are you giving it a fair chance? Have you exhausted all resources available to you to see if there are workable solutions to amend your complaints, whatever they may be?

Why and how did this happen? In the whirlwind (heck, typhoon-like) process of college selection, did you get sidetracked from your true preferences? Did you let your desire to go to a certain type of setting, university size, social life or curriculum fall by the wayside somehow? Did you only say "yes" because of pressure back home to attend this specific school? Did you *really* check out the school you accepted? Are you going to make the same mistakes in seeking out a transfer destination?

Did you get skunked? Did the view book or college administrators overstate or under-state the school's characteristics? Go back and look. This will give you a reality check on where you are now and help you plan better for the future. The idea is not to have the same thing happen again. If you do decide to transfer, make sure to question the colleges' PR spins so you can find a university that truly satisfies your needs.

You'll need a solid plan for next year. The actual process of transferring is considerable work. Make sure the institution you plan to attend will take you with the number of units you have. Some schools will only take transfer students with sophomore standing. Also find out how many transfer units your desired future institution will credit you with and put towards their requirements. This can be a nasty technical glitch that could spell a pro-tracted, expensive ride to graduation day or the tedium of retaking certain classes.

If you believe that you indeed made a mistake, then leave. It can be that simple. There is absolutely no stigma. Unnecessary misery is overrated, regardless. Transferring can provide an opportunity to start over and get the academic and social experience you deserve to have. Just do this with your eyes open. Research carefully and consider what you're after. If the problem lies deep inside of you, then it will follow you no matter how many schools you try. Last but not least, realize that there *is* life after transfer. The students on record here who finally took the big leap felt they had made the right decision.

● ●

CONCLUSION: *Thoughts to Live By*

I think I see a glimmer —
Into the woods — you have to grope,
But that's the way you learn to cope.
Into the woods to find there's hope
Of getting through the journey.

Into the woods, each time you go,
There's more to learn of what you know.
Into the woods, but not too slow —
Into the woods, it's nearing midnight —

Into the woods
To mind the wolf,
To heed the witch,
To honor the giant,
To mind,
To heed,
To find,
To think,
To teach,
To join,
To go to the Festival!

Into the woods,
Into the woods,
Into the woods,
Then out of the woods —
And happy ever after!

Finale from INTO THE WOODS,
Music and Lyrics by Stephen Sondheim

● ●

AFTERWORD: *Perspective for Parents*

One of the rewards you reap as parents of university students is having the opportunity to stand aside, just a little bit, and watch your children move into the wider world. Heading to college is one of life's highlights. Here your students will experience mixed feelings of excitement and fear, as being away from home presents them with the joys of independence, as well as the responsibilities of taking care of themselves.

As parents, you also have a new and often complicated set of feelings to sort out as your sons and daughters leave for college. Don't be surprised if you experience your own symptoms of separation anxiety.

It's important to remember that your students still need you as much as ever, only in a different way. Until now, you have been very involved with their day-to-day lives – their studies, social schedules, sleep habits, and nutrition. Now your students are legal adults with their own set of consequent rights and responsibilities. They are expected to handle their own affairs. But after all, this is what all your years of nurturing have been about – helping those small, dependent children mature into self-reliant, independent adults.

Rest assured, there is a wealth of academic, emotional, and physical support services to help them succeed. They just have to ask.

> *from* A Resource Guide for Parents
> *published by Cal Parents Program, Office of Public Affairs*
> *University of California, Berkeley*

• •

ACKNOWLEDGEMENTS: *In Order of Appearance*

Many thanks to all the young women we interviewed. They were the inspiration for the book. It was a privilege to meet them and spend time with them. The world is safe in their hands. We know it now. We are excited to see what the future will bring them, and what they will bring to the future.

Special thanks to Renee Barnett Terry, Ph.D., a true mentor, friend and gift. Learned. Wise. Very appreciated.

Thank you to our friends, family and educators. You took the time to read our efforts along the way, and gave us the best of your thinking. It helped! Tilman Borsch, Marlene Canter, Algerine Correia, Judy Cromwell, Kay Danelo, Holly Flor, John Gardner, Jenny Keup, Merrill Kruger, Morgan Kruger, Thomas Kruger, Whitney Landau, Isabel Leahey, Rudy Mangels, Eleanore Meyer, M.D., Peggy Poe, Gayle Simon, Pat Stanton, Jane Taber.

Thank you to our computer guru! Paul Kruger, Paul Kruger, Paul Kruger!

Special thanks to Sara Fisher, an editor with a fresh voice and a wide view. Her straightforward and thoughtful input was invaluable.

Special thanks to Jeanette Dvorak, a copyeditor with a gimlet eye and a graceful personality.

Appreciation for graphic assistance: Brian White. Patience, thy name is Brian.

Professional input, much appreciated: Paul Cassidy, Barbara Gottlieb, Kristin Odermatt, Laura Wiggins.

Final thanks. Several young women gave input and fresh insights as the project wound down. (Or up, depending on your point of view.) Paola Gilsanz, Meagan Kelliher, Emily Mazziotti, Lisa Thee, Cassie Unger.

To those we plain forgot to thank elsewhere. We appreciate you too. Please don't take our forgetfulness personally. It isn't intentional.

As far as errors. They're ours, you can bet on that.

• •

WHO'S WHO: *The Students*

The following is a partial list of the young women interviewed for this book. While each student is much, much more than test scores and alma mater types, this basic information gives greater insight into them, their backgrounds, and their perspectives. You can also scan for those who have made similar transitions as you, or see how those who have made totally different choices have fared. In some cases, where stories and background were similar, the young women interviewed were combined for simplicity. Each young woman selected her own alias.

The schools are identified by actual size and type. As far as school size and the question of how big is big; school sizes are indicated by undergraduate populations. Small: up to 3,000 students. Medium: 3,000 to 8,000. Large: 8,000 to 20,000. Very large: over 20,000. National ranking services were utilized to place the schools qualitatively.

ABBY
Year: sophomore
High school background: coed prep
College choice: small, top-tier liberal arts college transferring to large, top-tier private university
College application process: visited 11; applied to 5; accepted by 4
Vital stats: SAT 1210; high school GPA: 3.8; college GPA 3.6
Satisfaction with college choice: unhappy with choice, and transferred, eventually thrilled
Self-description: in high school: involved, happy, satisfied

ALEXANDRA
Year: sophomore
High school background: coed prep
College choice: small, top-tier liberal arts college
College application process: visited 20; applied to 8; accepted at 4
Vital stats: SAT 1290; high school GPA: 3.6; college GPA: 3.0
Satisfaction with college choice: satisfied+
Self-description: in high school: outgoing, artistic and athletic;
in college: independent, provocative, creative and artistic

ALLISON

Year: sophomore
High school background: coed prep
College choice: large, top-tier private university
College application process: visited 23; applied to 13; accepted by 10; 1 early action
Vital stats: SAT 1300; high school GPA: 3.8; college GPA: 3.4
Satisfaction with college choice: thrilled
Self-description: in high school: involved, happy, busy;
in college: happy, excited about school

AMBER

Year: sophomore
High school background: coed prep
College choice: very large, top-tier public university
College application process: visited 17; applied to 7; accepted by 3
Vital stats: SAT 1260; high school GPA: 3.7; college GPA 3.6
Satisfaction with college choice: thrilled
Self-description: in high school: energetic, active, outgoing;
in college: outgoing, determined, exploratory

ANN

Year: sophomore
High school background: coed prep
College choice: medium, top-tier private university
College application process: visited 7; applied to 7; accepted at 5
Vital stats: SAT 1560; high school GPA: 4.0+ college GPA: 3.9
Satisfaction with college choice: thrilled
Self-description: in high school: academically confident, socially unconfident, focused;
in college: happy, confident, free

ANNE B.

Year: freshman
High school background: coed prep
College choice: small, top-tier liberal arts women's college
College application process: visited 15; applied to 12; accepted by 9; waitlisted at 3
Vital stats: SAT 1530; high school GPA: 4.2; college GPA: uncertain
Self-description: in high school: mature, studious, content;
in college: so far, so good

ARIELLE
Year: freshman
High school background: all-girl parochial prep
College choice: very large, top-tier public university
College application process: applied to 6; accepted at 5
Vital stats: SAT 1400; high school GPA: 4.5; college GPA: uncertain
Satisfaction with college choice: thrilled
Self-description: in high-school: involved, peppy and friendly;
in college: dedicated, studious and fun

AYLA
Year: sophomore
High school background: all-girl parochial prep
College choice: large, top-tier public university to large, second-tier public university
College application process: visited 10; applied to 12; accepted by 6
Vital stats: SAT 1260; high school GPA: 3.9; college GPA: 2.8
Satisfaction with college choice: unhappy with choice and transferred; eventually thrilled.
Self-description: in high school: motivated, original, energetic;
in college: independent, brilliant, inventive

CHARLOTTE
Year: sophomore
High school background: coed prep
College choice: small, top-tier private university
College application process: visited 14; applied to 12; accepted by 9
Vital stats: SAT 1530; high school GPA: 4.2; college GPA: A's
Satisfaction with college choice: thrilled
Self-description: in high school: studious, driven, reserved;
in college: happy, involved, interested

HARRIET
Year: sophomore
High school background: coed prep
College choice: small, top-tier liberal arts college
College application process: visited 16; applied to 1; early decision
Vital stats: SAT 1450; high school GPA: 3.9; college GPA: 3.6
Satisfaction with college choice: thrilled, expectations met
Self-description: in high school: ambitious and shy;
in college: experimental, intellectual and fun-loving

HOLDEN
Year: freshman
High school background: coed prep
College choice: large, top-tier private university
College application process: visited 21; applied to 10; withdrew from 9 after early admission.
Vital stats: SAT 1300; high school GPA: 3.6; college GPA: uncertain
Satisfaction with college choice: thrilled, satisfied, expectations met
Self-description: in high school: involved, independent, happy constantly;
in college: happy, busy, learning

JANE
Year: freshman
High school background: all-girl prep
College choice: large, top-tier private university
College application process: visited 30; applied to 7; accepted by 6
Vital stats: SAT 1390; high school GPA: 3.2; college GPA: 3.7
Satisfaction with college choice: unhappy with choice, wanted to transfer
Self-description: in high school: goofy, clueless, tortured;
in college: unsure, confused, lacked direction

JENI
Year: sophomore
High school background: coed prep
College choice: very large, top-tier public university
College application process: visited 7; applied to 14; accepted at 7
Vital stats: SAT 1300; high school GPA: 3.4; college GPA: uncertain
Satisfaction with college choice: satisfied
Self-description: in high school: active;
in college: open and social

JOANNE
Year: sophomore
High school background: coed prep
College choice: medium, top-tier private university
College application process: visited 10; applied to 4; accepted early decision
Vital stats: SAT 1380; high school GPA: couldn't remember; college GPA: 3.1
Satisfaction with college choice: thrilled
Self-description: in high school: organized, focused, ambitious;
in college: independent, relaxed, happy

KAREN

Year: freshman
High school background: coed prep
College choice: small, top-tier liberal arts college
College application process: visited 26; applied to 11; accepted by 3
Vital stats: SAT 1300; high school GPA: 3.6; college GPA: unknown
Satisfaction with college choice: thrilled
Self-description: in high school: active, stressed;
in college: happy and active

KATE

Year: freshman
High school background: all-girl prep
College choice: large, top-tier public university
College application process: visited 8; applied to 12; accepted by 7
Satisfaction with college choice: thrilled, satisfied
Vital stats: SAT 1390; high school GPA: 3.7; college GPA 3.6
Self-description: in high school: studious, confident, inquisitive;
in college: outgoing, fun-oriented, interested in learning all that I can

LAUREN

Year: freshman
High school background: coed prep
College choice: medium, top-tier private university
College application process: visited 17; applied to 12; accepted at 10
Vital stats: SAT 1400; high school GPA: 4.4; college GPA: 3.9
Satisfaction with college choice: thrilled
Self-description: in high school: bright, artsy and fun;
in college; bright, artsy and fun

LEILA

Year: junior
High school background: all-girl prep
College choice: large, top-tier private university to community junior college
to very large public university (junior year)
College application process: visited 14; applied to 7; accepted by 4
Vital stats: SAT 1230; high school GPA: 3.9; college GPA: 3.0 to 3.5
Satisfaction with college choice: wanted to transfer
Self-description: in high school: outgoing, good friend, hard working;
in college: unhappy, confused, shaken self-confidence

LESLIE

Year: freshman
High school background: all-girl prep
College choice: medium-sized, top-tier private university
College application process: visited 27; accepted by 4 (1 early admission)
Vital stats: SAT 1470; high school GPA: 4.1; college GPA: NA
Satisfaction with college choice: thrilled
Self-description: Leslie was reluctant to limit herself to a three-word self-description.

LIBBY

Year: junior
High school background: coed prep
College choice: small, second-tier private university
College application process: visited 6; applied to 7; accepted by 2
Vital stats: SAT couldn't remember; high school GPA: couldn't remember; college GPA: dean's list first semester
Satisfaction with college choice: wanted to transfer
Self-description: in high school: dreamer, actor, bored;
in college: fun, dramatic, opinionated

LINDSAY

Year: sophomore
High school background: coed prep
College choice: medium, top-tier private university
College application process: visited 15; applied to 10; accepted at 5
Vital stats: SAT 1390; high school GPA: 3.9; college GPA: 3.6
Satisfaction with college choice: thrilled
Self-description: in high-school: determined, organized and fun;
in college: independent, imaginative and fun

LISA

Year: sophomore
High school background: all-girl prep
College choice: very large, top-tier public university
College application process: visited 16; applied to 9; accepted by 6
Vital stats: SAT 1330; high school GPA: 3.5; college GPA: 3.5
Satisfaction with college choice: thrilled
Self-description: in high school: quiet, funny, shy;
in college: talkative, confident, happy

LOLA

Year: sophomore
High school background: all-girl parochial prep
College choice: medium, top tier private university
College application process: visited 4; applied to 9; accepted by 5; waitlisted at 1
Vital stats: SAT 1410; high school GPA: 4.7; college GPA: 3.5
Satisfaction with college choice: thrilled
Self-description: in high school: busy, happy, hard working;
in college: happy, excited, motivated, interested

MEREDITH

Year: sophomore
High school background: coed prep
College choice: medium-sized, top-tier private university
College application process: visited 17; applied to 18; accepted by 9
Vital stats: SAT 1480; high school GPA: 4.3; college GPA 3.4
Satisfaction with college choice: thrilled.
Self-description: in high school: quiet, studious, energetic;
in college: outgoing, thoughtful, energetic

SAM

Year: sophomore
High school background: all-girl prep
College choice: medium, top-tier private university
College application process: visited 5; applied to 1; accepted by 1, early admission
Vital stats: SAT 1420; high school GPA: 3.6; college GPA: 3.2
Satisfaction with college choice: thrilled, satisfied, expectations met
Self-description: in high school: ambitious, self-absorbed and uncertain;
in college: brave, insightful and warm

SARA

Year: sophomore
High school background: all-girl prep
College choice: medium, top-tier private university
College application process: visited 10; applied to 8; accepted by 6
Vital stats: SAT 1350; high school GPA: 4.0; college GPA 3.8
Satisfaction with college choice: satisfied
Self-description: in high school: hardworking, tired, visible;
in college: more open to different people, less studious, independent

SCARLETT
Year: sophomore
High school background: all-girl prep
College choice: medium, top-tier private university
College application process: visited 10; applied to 11; accepted at 9
Vital stats: SAT 1440; high school GPA: 3.8; college GPA: 3.5
Satisfaction with college choice: thrilled
Self-description: in high school: busy, focused, introverted;
in college: busy and happy

SIMONE
Year: sophomore
High school background: all-girl prep
College choice: medium, top-tier private university
College application process: visited 18; applied to 8; accepted by 7
Vital stats: SAT 1450; high school GPA: 3.9; college GPA: unknown
Satisfaction with college choice: thrilled
Self-description: in high school: driven, involved, socially reserved;
in college: happy, excited, determined

SOPHIE
Year: sophomore
High school background: coed prep
College choice: medium, top-tier private university
College application process: visited 19; applied to 8; accepted at 7
Vital stats: SAT 1360; high school GPA: 3.8; college GPA: 3.5
Satisfaction with college choice: satisfied
Self-description: in high school: studious, friendly and fun;
in college: studious, silly, less stressed

STEPHANIE
Year: sophomore
High school background: coed prep
College choice: medium, top tier private university
College application process: visited 18; applied to 7; accepted by 7
Vital stats: SAT 1400; high school GPA: 3.8; college GPA: 3.0
Satisfaction with college choice: satisfied
Self-description: in high school: different, active, just there;
in college: tired, excited, calm but anxious

SYDNEY
Year: sophomore
High school background: all-girl prep
College choice: medium, top-tier private university
College application process: visited 23, applied to 15; accepted by 14
Vital stats: SAT 1470; high school GPA: 4.2; college GPA: 3.0
Satisfaction with college choice: expectations met
Self-description: in high school: energetic, hardworking, innovative;
in college: innovative, adaptable, playful

VICTORIA
Year: sophomore
High school background: coed prep
College choice: very large, top-tier national university
College application process: visited 8; applied to 10; accepted at 6
Vital stats: SAT doesn't remember; high school GPA: 4.1; college GPA: uncertain
Satisfaction with college choice: satisfied
Self-description: in high school: involved, clever, studious;
in college: fun, studious, philosophical

Appendix B

● ●

RESEARCH METHODS: *How We Did It*

This book was born out of overpowering curiosity: What exactly happens to the young women who march off to American colleges every fall? The short answer is that they change. That much is clear. But how, precisely? In what ways, exactly? What challenges should students who teeter on the brink of college be prepared for? How can parents best help their children help themselves as they prepare to fly the nest?

We set off to find out the answers to these burning questions, armed with an elegantly simple plan.

We asked.

Well, it took two years – a lot longer than we had planned – but it was an immensely informative and enjoyable process. With one student at a time, we sat down in one of half a dozen Starbucks (bless that company and their incredibly patient employees!) and mulled things over with a latte or a cappuccino for a couple hours or so. Generally, both of us as authors participated in all the interviews. The sessions were guided by a nine-page, two-part questionnaire we created especially for the book, with the help of educators, parents and students.

The first part of the questionnaire placed the interviewees in their context: name, rank and serial number, so to speak, including the nature of their college, size of family and previous experiences away from home. The second part tackled the more subjective issues such as feelings about roommates, classes and, ummm, er, - social habits. As it turned out, this second section provided a springboard to far-ranging discussions that in fact brought up much more personal issues than we would have ever had the nerve to ask point blank.

Each young woman interviewed was promised confidentiality, which provided the kind of safety net needed to encourage (*really*) unbelievable candor. They selected their own aliases and are not identified with their particular college or university. We also took the time to visit a dozen or more of the campuses personally.

So whom did we interview and where did they go to school?

The students were mostly college freshmen and sophomores, with a few juniors thrown into the mix. We started by casting a wide net, identifying and contacting over 200 possible candidates. Each had attended a top-notch high school, usually an independent or parochial college prep school. And each had been accepted at a top-notch private or public U.S. university with an excellent reputation for retaining their freshman class and graduating that class in four or slightly more years.

You will find the interviewees' profiles in the preceding appendix. All were simply great young adults. The schools they attended included (in part) Brown, Columbia, Cornell, Duke, Harvard, Northwestern, NYU, Princeton, Swarthmore, Stanford, U.C. Berkeley, U.C. Los Angeles, U.C. San Diego, U. Michigan, U. Pennsylvania, Washington University, Wesleyan, Williams, and Yale.

After the initial contact, a smaller number of young women were interviewed in person, and finally there were follow-ups via telephone and e-mail.

We acknowledge that our chosen sample of students is specialized, and certainly doesn't reflect the entire range of high schoolers marching off to college. But that's not what this book is about. We approached this project with the assumption (hypothesis, if you want to get more technical) that when well-prepared students attend a top-quality college –where there is a history of the freshman class staying put – most academic issues (poor preparation, inadequate class content and the like) are minimized – at least for their lower-classmen years. This leaves the other issues that make freshman year so emotionally dramatic free to float to the surface uncrowded. Can this assumption be argued? Certainly. But it seemed like a good starting place, especially since no one else seemed to be asking these questions in such a qualitative and personal way.

One question frequently put to us is, wasn't it difficult to track down all these students, a notoriously transient population? The answer is yes. But it was also easier than it could have been since we had years (make that decades!) as parents learning about this particular cohort of young people. While we did not personally know the majority of the young women whose experiences appear in these pages, friends, acquaintances and educators helped us develop a list of their names and the colleges.

This book is driven by the women's topics and their quotes. Reviewing the questionnaires revealed about 15 topics that were almost universally discussed. Roommates, guys, Greek life, academics and food were most frequently mentioned. One of our most surprising discoveries was the common topic of returning home as a source of conflict.

Once we identified our key themes, quotes were selected that best reflected the range of feelings for each topic. Not surprisingly, there was quite a bit of repetition among the women's experiences and advice, so we culled our sources down to a smaller list of contributors. In a few cases stories were combined in order to tell a fuller story, but we were *extremely* careful to remain faithful to the young women's input. We feel that we have very accurately represented the spirit and the letter of the interviewees' ideas and words.

As the book moved along through its various stages of development, it underwent some peer review. These generous readers included groups of young women and young men who had not participated in the interviews, mothers of high school seniors or college freshmen, college counselors and friends.

While we realized early on that the transition to college *was* a shock for most of the students interviewed, these are absolutely stories of success. Problems were faced and dealt with. With one exception, every young woman interviewed was still in college and progressing toward her degree as this book goes to print.

Our goal here was to present in an entertaining and readable format the conflicts and experiences faced by young women their first year in college. At its core, this is a book of discovery about a journey taken every year by young people throughout America. These women are very fortunate. And we are too, to have met them.

● ●

ABOUT THE AUTHORS

Sally Landau and Val Holwerda are parents of teenagers. Their lives and homes are filled with dozens of teens and families facing and navigating the college challenge. Sally has a B.A. in Psychology. Val has a B.A. in Literature and an M.B.A. They have been writing partners and friends for more than a decade.

● ●

QUICK ORDER FORM

Order by Telephone: 800.844.3032 Please have your credit card ready.
 For quantity orders, see (*) below.

By Fax: 914.835.0398 or 310.454.6474. Send this form.

By Mail: Bristol Press Inc. Box 49958, Los Angeles CA 90049

By E-mail: bookch@aol.com

Name: _____

Street Address: _____

_____

City: _____ **State:** _____ **Zip:**_____

Telephone: (____)_____E-mail Address:_____

Please send _____ copies of <u>College Shock</u>
 to the address above at $16.95 each. $_____
 Use a separate sheet for additional address(es).

Sales Tax: Add 8.25% for books shipped to CA addresses. $_____

Shipping: We ship by Priority Mail.
            $4 for the first book, $2 for each additional book.
            Call for additional options. $_____

                              Total enclosed: $_____

Payment: ___Check or money order enclosed

           ___Credit Card: Visa or Mastercard (circle one)

            Card Number:_____Exp:_____

            Name on Card: _____

            Signature (Required): _____

<u>College Shock</u> is on the web at **www.promaris.com**

Quantity pricing and custom editions available.
 Contact Bristol Press at 310.719.4053 for information.